EFFECTIVE
LEADERSHIP

A Guide to Unlocking the Art of Leadership

RAY HOWELL

CONTENTS

DEDICATION
To all those who inspire through their actions, lead with empathy, and make a difference in the lives of others. To the mentors and visionaries who shape the future by investing in people, encouraging growth, and fostering resilience. And to every aspiring leader who dares to step forward with courage, embrace the responsibility, and unlock the transformative power within themselves. This book is for you.

FOREWORD

In today's world, effective leadership is more than a title or position—it is a journey of self-discovery, growth, and purposeful influence. The most impactful leaders are not only those who achieve great results but those who uplift others, foster collaboration, and leave a legacy of positive change. *Effective Leadership: A Guide for Unlocking the Art of Leadership* is a timely exploration of the qualities, principles, and skills that define exceptional leaders. It is a guide not only for those at the pinnacle of their careers but also for anyone on the path to realizing their full leadership potential.

This book breaks down the art and science of leadership into actionable insights that are relevant across industries, fields, and stages of life. It addresses everything from core leadership principles and effective communication to team building, ethical decision-making, and adaptability. Each chapter is designed to equip readers with the knowledge to lead authentically, make sound decisions, and build resilient teams.

In a world constantly reshaped by change, the ability to lead with adaptability, empathy, and integrity is crucial. As a reader, you will not only gain insights into different leadership styles but will also learn to recognize your own strengths and areas for growth. This book is a reminder that leadership is a continual journey, one that requires a commitment to self-improvement and a willingness to learn from others.

Whether you are a seasoned leader, a new manager, or someone simply passionate about making an impact, *Effective Leadership* offers a roadmap for navigating the complexities of leadership in the modern era. It challenges you to consider what kind of leader you wish to be and provides the tools to help you make that vision a reality.

As you turn these pages, may you be inspired to lead with purpose, humility, and an unwavering commitment to those you serve. The world needs leaders who can not only adapt but also inspire transformation in others. This book, rich with insights and wisdom, is a valuable resource on that journey.

INTRODUCTION

The nature of leadership is complex, dynamic, and continuously evolving. As we enter an era marked by rapid changes in technology, global challenges, and shifting workplace expectations, effective leadership has never been more crucial. In its truest form, leadership is not just about holding authority or giving directives; it is about inspiring others to realize a shared vision and empowering them to grow. This book, *Effective Leadership: A Guide for Unlocking the Art of Leadership*, is designed to be a comprehensive and practical resource for anyone aspiring to become a more impactful leader. Through this guide, we will explore both the foundational and nuanced aspects of leadership, offering tools and insights that can be applied in any context—whether you're leading a team, an organization, or your own journey of personal development.

UNDERSTANDING LEADERSHIP

Leadership is often defined by influence, motivation, and vision. Yet, true leadership goes beyond mere definitions; it requires a deep understanding of self, others, and the purpose behind one's actions. At its core, leadership is about creating change and achieving results through people. Effective leaders are those who can mobilize and inspire others towards a common goal, fostering an environment where individuals feel valued and are encouraged to contribute their unique strengths.

Leadership is a relationship between the leader and the people they are leading. It is a process of building trust, respect, and alignment. A leader must be able to understand the aspirations and concerns of their team, providing guidance and support while encouraging independence and innovation. Importantly, leadership is not restricted to formal roles. Anyone can demonstrate leadership through actions that inspire, guide, or support others. In today's interconnected world, this kind of distributed leadership is vital as it empowers individuals at all levels to contribute to meaningful outcomes.

THE EVOLUTION OF LEADERSHIP THEORY

The study of leadership has evolved dramatically over the centuries. Early theories tended to focus on the characteristics or traits that distinguished leaders from non-leaders, known as the *Great Man Theory*. This approach suggested that leadership was an innate quality, something individuals were born with. Over time, however, the understanding of leadership shifted. Behavioral theories emerged, emphasizing that leadership could be learned, with specific behaviors and skills contributing to effective leadership.

In the 20th century, the *Situational and Contingency Theories* proposed that there is no one-size-fits-all approach to leadership; instead, effective leaders adapt their style according to the context and the people they are leading. This shift laid the groundwork for more flexible and adaptive leadership models, such as *Transformational Leadership*, which highlights the role of leaders in inspiring and empowering their teams, and *Servant Leadership*, which focuses on prioritizing the needs of others.

Recent decades have introduced theories that emphasize emotional intelligence, ethics, and social responsibility in leadership. The rise of *Adaptive Leadership* reflects a world where leaders must be flexible, innovative, and resilient in response to constant change. This theory underscores the importance of leaders not only managing change but also guiding their organizations and teams through it, helping them thrive in challenging environments.

By understanding the evolution of these theories, leaders gain a broader perspective on the various approaches they can employ and the adaptability needed to meet contemporary challenges. Today's leaders benefit from a rich legacy of ideas that encourage them to lead with empathy, responsibility, and foresight.

PURPOSE AND SCOPE OF THIS GUIDE

Effective Leadership is not just a theoretical exploration; it is a practical guide for leaders at every stage. This book aims to provide readers with actionable insights into the art and science of leadership, covering both foundational concepts and advanced techniques. From understanding personal values to mastering communication, building teams, and leading through change, this guide offers a comprehensive roadmap for developing leadership skills.

The purpose of this guide is twofold: to help individuals become more self-aware and intentional in their leadership and to provide a toolkit for effectively managing and inspiring others. We recognize that leadership is a personal journey, one that requires continuous growth, reflection, and adaptation. This book seeks to support that journey, equipping readers with the knowledge and skills needed to navigate the complexities of leadership in a rapidly evolving world.

This guide is not limited to those in executive roles; it is designed for anyone with a desire to make a positive impact, whether in a corporate setting, community organization, or even personal relationships. Each chapter is carefully crafted to help readers develop both the inner qualities and practical skills that define an effective leader.

KEY TRAITS OF EFFECTIVE LEADERS

While each leader brings unique qualities to their role, there are certain traits that are consistently associated with effective leadership. These traits go beyond technical skills or expertise; they are the interpersonal qualities and behaviors that inspire trust, respect, and commitment from others.

1. **Vision**: Effective leaders have a clear sense of purpose and direction. They are able to articulate a compelling vision of the future and inspire others to work toward that vision. This requires foresight, creativity, and the ability to see beyond immediate challenges.

2. **Integrity**: Trustworthiness and honesty are at the heart of effective leadership. Leaders with integrity are consistent in their values and actions, which builds trust with their teams. They lead by example, uphold ethical standards, and take responsibility for their actions.

3. **Emotional Intelligence**: The ability to understand and manage one's own emotions, as well as empathize with others, is essential for effective leadership. Leaders with high emotional intelligence are better equipped to handle conflicts, build relationships, and create a positive work environment.

4. **Resilience**: In the face of adversity, effective leaders remain steady and composed. Resilience enables leaders to navigate challenges, setbacks, and

uncertainties without losing sight of their goals. It also instills confidence in their team, showing that obstacles can be overcome.

5. **Adaptability**: With the pace of change in today's world, leaders must be able to adapt quickly to new situations and evolving circumstances. Adaptable leaders are open to new ideas, embrace change, and continuously seek improvement, both for themselves and their organizations.

6. **Communication Skills**: Effective leaders are clear, persuasive, and inspiring communicators. They understand that leadership is as much about listening as it is about speaking, and they use communication to foster alignment, clarity, and mutual respect within their teams.

7. **Empathy**: Empathy allows leaders to understand the experiences and emotions of others. Empathetic leaders are approachable, supportive, and able to connect on a human level, which fosters loyalty and respect among their team members.

8. **Accountability**: Great leaders take responsibility for their actions and decisions, and they hold themselves and their teams accountable. Accountability builds a culture of trust and transparency, reinforcing a commitment to high standards and ethical behavior.

9. **Innovation**: Leaders are often required to think creatively and bring fresh perspectives to problem-solving. An innovative leader fosters a culture of creativity, encouraging their team to take calculated risks, explore new ideas, and drive meaningful change.

10. **Commitment to Growth**: Effective leaders recognize that learning is a lifelong journey. They invest in their own development and encourage growth in others, building a culture where continuous improvement is

valued and pursued.

In this guide, we will explore each of these traits in depth, examining how they contribute to effective leadership and providing practical advice on how to cultivate them. By developing these qualities, readers will not only enhance their own leadership capabilities but also foster a more collaborative, inspired, and resilient environment for those they lead.

CHAPTER 1: THE FOUNDATION OF LEADERSHIP

At the heart of every successful organization, team, or movement lies effective leadership. Leadership is not merely a role or position; it is the cornerstone of progress, the guiding force that drives people toward a shared goal, and the influence that shapes a positive environment for growth and productivity. This chapter dives into the foundational elements of leadership, covering its core principles, the importance of vision, mission, and values, the role of emotional intelligence, and the essential task of building trust and credibility. Together, these elements form the bedrock of effective leadership, enabling leaders to inspire, influence, and achieve meaningful results.

DEFINING LEADERSHIP AND ITS CORE PRINCIPLES

Leadership is the art and science of guiding others to achieve a common goal. While often associated with authority and control, true leadership transcends these traditional views. Effective leadership is about influence, vision, and collaboration rather than power alone. Leaders shape a path forward, motivate their teams, and foster an environment where everyone feels empowered to contribute.

Core principles of leadership include:

1. **Influence Over Authority**: Leadership is about inspiring others rather than simply directing them. A leader's influence stems from respect, trust, and credibility rather than just positional power. Influence encourages buy-in, commitment, and a shared vision.

2. **Servitude and Responsibility**: Leaders view themselves as servants to the cause and their team, placing the needs of others above their own. This principle, often associated with *Servant Leadership*, emphasizes that a leader's role is to empower and support their team.

3. **Empowerment and Growth**: Leaders don't just direct people; they enable them to grow. Effective leaders are mentors and coaches who recognize and nurture potential within their team members. This principle is

rooted in the belief that leadership is about creating more leaders, not followers.

4. **Adaptability and Resilience**: Change is constant, and leadership requires a willingness to adapt. Resilient leaders remain steady in the face of challenges, demonstrating flexibility and problem-solving abilities to help their teams navigate uncertainty.

5. **Vision and Integrity**: Leadership is ultimately about guiding people toward a vision of what could be. A leader's integrity—honesty, ethical behavior, and consistency—instills trust in their team, encouraging them to follow the leader's vision wholeheartedly.

Together, these principles define the essence of leadership. They are not merely theoretical but are qualities that leaders must embody in their everyday interactions. Leadership is not defined by one's title; it is demonstrated through actions, decisions, and the impact one has on others.

VISION, MISSION, AND VALUES

A leader's vision, mission, and values are like a compass, giving direction and purpose to their efforts. These three elements clarify why the organization or team exists, what it hopes to accomplish, and how it will operate along the way.

1. **Vision**: A vision is a clear, compelling idea of what the future could look like. It's an aspirational statement that reflects the leader's long-term goals for the team or organization. A powerful vision provides a sense of purpose, a reason for people to unite and work toward something greater than themselves. A leader's vision should be inspiring, realistic, and achievable, encouraging others to commit to the journey.

2. **Mission**: The mission outlines what the team or organization does, its primary goals, and its target audience. While the vision speaks to the future, the mission addresses the present—what actions need to be taken daily to move closer to that vision. An effective mission statement gives clarity and focus, ensuring that everyone understands their purpose and how they contribute to the greater objective.

3. **Values**: Values are the guiding principles that shape the way a team or organization operates. They represent the standards of behavior and attitudes that are prioritized, such as honesty, respect, and innovation. Values serve as the moral foundation,

influencing every decision, interaction, and goal. They also reinforce the culture, defining "how" work is done and setting expectations for behavior and performance.

A leader must establish and communicate these elements effectively. Vision, mission, and values are not just words on paper; they should be evident in the leader's actions, decisions, and communication. By aligning the team's daily activities with these core elements, leaders create a sense of cohesion, unity, and shared purpose that motivates people to work towards common goals.

THE ROLE OF EMOTIONAL INTELLIGENCE

Emotional intelligence (EI) is the ability to recognize, understand, and manage one's own emotions, as well as empathize with and influence the emotions of others. In leadership, EI is critical because it directly affects a leader's ability to build relationships, handle stress, and communicate effectively. Daniel Goleman, a leading psychologist and EI researcher, identified five main components of emotional intelligence that are essential for effective leadership:

1. **Self-Awareness**: Self-awareness is the foundation of emotional intelligence. Leaders who are self-aware understand their strengths, weaknesses, values, and motivations. This awareness allows them to manage their reactions and make thoughtful decisions, even in challenging situations. Self-aware leaders are humble and open to feedback, which fosters a culture of honesty and continuous improvement.

2. **Self-Regulation**: Effective leaders can manage their emotions and remain calm under pressure. Self-regulation is about controlling impulsive responses and handling emotions constructively. Leaders who practice self-regulation avoid acting out of anger or frustration, instead responding thoughtfully to situations. This steadiness under stress helps to

maintain team morale and sets a positive example.

3. **Motivation**: Leaders with high emotional intelligence are motivated by internal rewards, such as a passion for their work or a commitment to a cause, rather than just external rewards like money or recognition. This intrinsic motivation drives leaders to work hard, set ambitious goals, and inspire others with their dedication and work ethic.

4. **Empathy**: Empathy is the ability to understand and share the feelings of others. In leadership, empathy is essential for building strong, trusting relationships. Empathetic leaders listen actively, consider others' perspectives, and are sensitive to their needs. By showing genuine concern, they create a supportive environment where people feel valued and understood.

5. **Social Skills**: Social skills are the abilities needed to communicate, influence, and build relationships effectively. Leaders with strong social skills are adept at managing conflicts, collaborating with others, and building networks. They are skilled at reading social cues and adjusting their communication to resonate with different individuals, making them effective communicators and relationship builders.

Emotional intelligence allows leaders to create a supportive and respectful environment, enhancing team dynamics and fostering a culture of open communication. Leaders who master EI can lead with empathy, resilience, and understanding, building teams that are motivated, cohesive, and resilient.

BUILDING TRUST AND CREDIBILITY

Trust and credibility are the cornerstones of effective leadership. When people trust a leader, they are more willing to follow, collaborate, and commit to shared goals. Trust is built through consistent actions, integrity, and a genuine concern for others' well-being, while credibility is established through expertise, reliability, and consistency.

1. **Consistency and Reliability**: Trust is developed when a leader's actions align with their words. Leaders who are dependable, who follow through on commitments, and who consistently act in accordance with their stated values build credibility over time. Consistency also creates a sense of security among team members, as they know they can rely on their leader's guidance and support.

2. **Transparency and Honesty**: Effective leaders are transparent in their communication. They openly share information, admit mistakes, and acknowledge areas for improvement. Honest communication fosters a sense of integrity and authenticity, which, in turn, strengthens trust. A leader who is upfront about challenges and open to feedback creates an environment where others feel comfortable being honest and vulnerable.

3. **Competence and Expertise**: Leaders gain credibility through knowledge and expertise. A leader who

understands the intricacies of their field, possesses problem-solving skills, and can make informed decisions is more likely to earn the respect of their team. Competence reassures team members that their leader is equipped to guide them effectively.

4. **Empathy and Support**: Trust is fostered through genuine relationships. Leaders who show empathy, listen actively, and support their team's personal and professional growth build deep connections. This support fosters loyalty, as team members feel valued not just as employees but as individuals.

5. **Accountability**: A credible leader takes responsibility for their actions and decisions. By holding themselves accountable, leaders demonstrate integrity and set an example for others. Accountability also includes recognizing and addressing one's mistakes, showing that the leader is committed to fairness and continuous improvement.

Building trust and credibility is not a one-time task but an ongoing commitment. Leaders must consistently demonstrate their values, integrity, and reliability through their everyday actions. When trust and credibility are established, teams become more cohesive, resilient, and engaged, working together effectively to achieve shared goals.

This chapter explores the foundational elements of effective leadership, starting with a clear understanding of leadership itself and the principles that underpin it. Vision, mission, and values provide direction, emotional intelligence fosters strong relationships, and trust and credibility solidify the leader's influence. Each of these foundational elements is essential for cultivating a leadership style that inspires, motivates, and drives meaningful change. As we move forward in this guide, we'll build upon these foundations to delve into more advanced aspects of leadership, equipping readers with the tools and insights needed to lead with confidence, empathy, and purpose.

CHAPTER 2: LEADERSHIP STYLES AND WHEN TO USE THEM

Leadership isn't a one-size-fits-all approach. Different situations, teams, and goals require leaders to adapt their style to best guide and motivate their team. This chapter explores the major leadership styles, including Situational Leadership, Transformational and Transactional Leadership, and Servant Leadership. Understanding these styles allows leaders to apply the right approach based on the needs of their team, the demands of the moment, and the desired outcomes. We'll also dive into practical examples to illustrate each style and offer guidance on when each might be most effective.

OVERVIEW OF LEADERSHIP STYLES

Leadership styles refer to the characteristic approaches and methods leaders use to guide, motivate, and manage their teams. Each style comes with its unique strengths, as well as specific situations where it excels. Broadly, leadership styles can be categorized as follows:

1. **Authoritative Leadership**: This style is about control and decision-making. The leader sets a clear vision and directs the team towards it, making most of the decisions themselves. It's effective in high-stakes environments but can stifle creativity if overused.

2. **Democratic Leadership**: Also known as participative leadership, this style involves input from team members in decision-making. It fosters collaboration and inclusivity, but it can slow down decision-making when quick responses are needed.

3. **Laissez-Faire Leadership**: Here, the leader takes a hands-off approach, allowing team members autonomy in how they work. This style works well when the team is highly skilled, but it can lead to a lack of direction and accountability if not managed carefully.

4. **Transactional Leadership**: Focused on rewards and punishments, this style relies on clear structures and defined roles. It's useful for achieving short-term goals and managing routine tasks, but it may not encourage

long-term growth or creativity.

5. **Transformational Leadership**: This approach focuses on inspiring and motivating teams by providing a vision for the future and encouraging personal growth. It's effective for driving change and innovation but can require significant energy and emotional investment from the leader.

6. **Servant Leadership**: A service-oriented style, where the leader prioritizes the well-being and development of their team members. It builds trust and loyalty, though it may be challenging when quick, decisive action is required.

Each of these styles offers a different approach to leadership, and often, the best leaders blend aspects of multiple styles to fit the situation and team dynamic.

SITUATIONAL LEADERSHIP

Situational Leadership is a flexible approach developed by Paul Hersey and Ken Blanchard. It posits that there's no single "best" style of leadership; instead, effective leaders adapt their approach based on the specific situation and the development level of their team members. Situational leadership is characterized by four primary styles, each suited to different scenarios:

1. **Directing**: In this style, the leader provides clear instructions and closely supervises tasks. It's best suited for team members who are new to a role or lack confidence, as they need high levels of guidance. For example, a manager leading a group of interns might use a directing style to ensure they understand each task step-by-step.

2. **Coaching**: Here, the leader offers guidance but also encourages input from team members. This style is useful for individuals who have some level of competence but still need support to gain full confidence. For instance, a leader working with an employee who is learning a new system may use coaching to answer questions, offer suggestions, and encourage them to problem-solve independently.

3. **Supporting**: The supporting style allows team members to make more decisions independently, while the leader provides encouragement and support.

It's best for individuals who are competent but may lack confidence. An example might be a project manager overseeing a skilled team that needs occasional feedback but is otherwise capable of working autonomously.

4. **Delegating**: In this style, the leader hands over responsibility and decision-making to the team. This approach works well for highly competent, motivated team members who require minimal supervision. For example, a senior analyst might be given full responsibility for a project's strategic direction, with the leader only checking in at key milestones.

The benefit of situational leadership is that it allows leaders to respond to the changing needs of their team, encouraging development by adjusting their support and guidance accordingly.

TRANSFORMATIONAL VS. TRANSACTIONAL LEADERSHIP

Transformational Leadership and **Transactional Leadership** represent two distinct ends of the leadership spectrum.

Transformational Leadership

Transformational leaders inspire and motivate their team by creating a compelling vision for the future, encouraging personal growth, and fostering a sense of purpose. They prioritize big-picture thinking and long-term goals, often challenging team members to step outside their comfort zones.

Example: Consider a leader in a tech company who rallies their team around a vision of revolutionizing an industry with a new, cutting-edge product. This leader encourages employees to experiment, even if it involves taking risks, and provides opportunities for professional development. The leader might hold weekly brainstorming sessions to fuel creativity and help team members see how their contributions fit into the larger mission. The result is a highly motivated team, eager to innovate and push boundaries.

Transformational leadership works best in environments where change and innovation are priorities, such as tech companies, start-ups, or organizations undergoing significant transformation.

Transactional Leadership

In contrast, transactional leadership is focused on structure, order, and achieving specific, short-term goals. Transactional leaders use a system of rewards and consequences to manage performance, which can be highly effective for routine, task-oriented environments.

Example: A transactional leader might manage a customer service team, setting specific performance targets for call response times, quality scores, and customer satisfaction ratings. Employees who meet their goals may receive bonuses, while those who don't may be required to undergo additional training. This style is useful when the goal is to meet defined objectives and maintain consistent performance standards.

Transactional leadership is especially effective in environments where tasks are routine, and consistent results are essential, such as in manufacturing, sales, or call centers.

SERVANT LEADERSHIP: PUTTING OTHERS FIRST

Servant Leadership is a philosophy where the leader's primary goal is to serve their team, focusing on the growth and well-being of their people before their own ambitions. This style, coined by Robert K. Greenleaf, is based on the idea that leaders should act as mentors and advocates, prioritizing empathy, compassion, and community building.

In servant leadership, the leader invests in their team's development, well-being, and satisfaction, often leading from a place of humility. Servant leaders create an environment where team members feel valued, understood, and empowered to reach their potential.

Example: A nonprofit organization might have a servant leader who works alongside volunteers, offering support, encouragement, and resources to help them accomplish the organization's mission. This leader spends time understanding each volunteer's strengths and areas of interest, assigning them tasks that align with their passions. The result is a motivated, loyal team that feels appreciated and committed to the cause.

Servant leadership is effective in environments where team morale, well-being, and collaboration are critical, such as in nonprofits, education, or health care. It's especially useful when the goal is to foster a strong sense of community and support.

CHOOSING THE RIGHT STYLE FOR DIFFERENT CONTEXTS

An effective leader recognizes that different situations require different leadership styles. A key aspect of adaptive leadership is the ability to evaluate a situation and select the approach that best meets the needs of the team and objectives at hand. Here are some guidelines for selecting the right leadership style for various contexts:

1. **In Times of Crisis**: In high-stress situations where quick decisions are essential, an authoritative or directing style can be effective. For example, during a financial downturn, a company CEO might need to make rapid decisions and communicate a clear plan without extensive team consultation.

2. **When Developing New Employees**: Situational leadership styles, like directing and coaching, are helpful for onboarding new team members. This approach provides the guidance and support necessary as they gain confidence and learn their roles.

3. **For High-Performing Teams**: With experienced and skilled teams, a delegating or laissez-faire approach can encourage autonomy and innovation. For instance, a research and development team working on new technology might thrive under a hands-off leader who provides resources and direction but allows

them freedom in execution.

4. **In a Creative or Innovative Environment**: Transformational leadership can be powerful when the objective is to inspire creativity and drive long-term innovation. Leaders in advertising, product design, or start-ups often benefit from a transformational approach that fosters big thinking and encourages team members to challenge the status quo.

5. **In Routine, Task-Oriented Roles**: Transactional leadership is effective for tasks with specific, measurable outcomes, such as in sales or production environments. It provides clear expectations and incentives, motivating employees to achieve short-term objectives.

6. **When Building Team Morale and Trust**: Servant leadership is effective for creating a culture of trust, respect, and mutual support. It's ideal in fields that require close collaboration, like social work or healthcare, where team members may benefit from a strong support system and a leader who genuinely cares about their well-being.

Summary

This chapter has explored the different leadership styles and the contexts in which each style is most effective. From situational flexibility to transformational inspiration, transactional order, and servant leadership's empathy, each approach has its place in the leader's toolkit. Great leaders understand that leadership is dynamic, adapting their style based on the goals, team dynamics, and challenges at hand. This adaptability not only maximizes effectiveness but also fosters a supportive, results-driven culture that can thrive in various circumstances.

CHAPTER 3: COMMUNICATION SKILLS FOR LEADERS

Effective communication is at the core of leadership. The ability to clearly convey messages, actively listen, handle difficult conversations, and resolve conflicts is essential for leaders who want to inspire and guide their teams. In this chapter, we explore key communication skills for leaders, from active listening to conflict resolution, along with examples to illustrate how these skills can be effectively applied.

THE ART OF ACTIVE LISTENING

Active listening goes beyond simply hearing what someone is saying; it involves being fully present, understanding the message, and responding thoughtfully. Leaders who practice active listening build trust, create open lines of communication, and demonstrate respect for their team members. It helps ensure that team members feel valued and understood, which can enhance morale and productivity.

1. **Techniques for Active Listening**:
   - **Maintain Eye Contact**: Showing genuine interest by maintaining eye contact demonstrates attentiveness and engagement.
   - **Avoid Interrupting**: Let the person finish speaking before responding, which shows respect for their thoughts.
   - **Ask Open-Ended Questions**: Use questions that encourage elaboration and provide deeper insight, like, "Can you tell me more about how you feel this will impact the project?"
   - **Paraphrase and Summarize**: Repeat back or summarize what the person has said to confirm understanding. For instance, "So, you're saying that the deadline feels too tight due to the additional workload. Is that correct?"

2. **Example**: Imagine a leader in a customer service department whose team is feeling overwhelmed due to an increase in call volume. Instead of immediately suggesting solutions, the leader listens to each team member's concerns individually. By actively listening, the leader learns that employees feel more stressed because of unclear call-handling guidelines. This insight allows the leader to create a clear guideline document, effectively reducing stress and increasing efficiency.

Active listening helps leaders understand the root cause of issues, provides validation to team members, and ultimately leads to better-informed decisions.

CRAFTING CLEAR AND EFFECTIVE MESSAGES

Clear and concise communication is crucial for leaders. Messages that are ambiguous or overly complex can lead to confusion, mistakes, and reduced morale. Crafting effective messages involves being direct, using simple language, and tailoring the message to the audience.

1. **Steps to Craft Clear Messages**:
    - **Know the Objective**: Before communicating, identify the purpose of the message. Is it to inform, request action, or provide feedback?
    - **Use Simple Language**: Avoid jargon or technical terms that may confuse others unless you're certain everyone understands them.
    - **Be Concise**: Short, to-the-point messages are often more impactful and easier for recipients to remember.
    - **Provide Context**: Explain the "why" behind a message to ensure team members understand its importance.

2. **Example**: A project manager needs to inform the team about a new deadline. Instead of saying, "We need to accelerate our timeline due to unforeseen factors," the manager could say, "The project deadline has moved up by two weeks to meet our client's needs. Let's meet tomorrow to adjust our schedule and determine next

steps." This message is clear, provides context, and sets the stage for a collaborative response.

Effective messaging minimizes misunderstandings, improves team alignment, and keeps everyone focused on shared objectives.

HANDLING DIFFICULT CONVERSATIONS

Difficult conversations are inevitable in leadership. These may involve giving constructive feedback, addressing performance issues, or navigating interpersonal conflicts. A leader who handles tough conversations with empathy, respect, and clarity can turn potentially negative experiences into opportunities for growth and improvement.

1. **Strategies for Difficult Conversations**:
   - **Prepare in Advance**: Understand the issue, gather relevant facts, and consider possible reactions from the individual.
   - **Use "I" Statements**: Framing feedback from your perspective (e.g., "I noticed that deadlines were missed...") can prevent the other person from feeling attacked.
   - **Focus on Solutions**: Instead of dwelling on the problem, discuss actionable steps for improvement. For example, "I think we can work together on ways to manage the workload more effectively."
   - **Remain Calm and Composed**: Keep emotions in check, even if the other person becomes defensive.

2. **Example**: A manager must address an employee whose performance has been slipping. Instead of saying, "You're not meeting expectations," the manager could

say, "I've noticed some changes in your performance, and I'd like to understand if there's anything going on that I can help with." This approach opens the door for an honest conversation and allows the employee to share any challenges they may be facing, making it easier to find a constructive solution.

Handling difficult conversations with sensitivity can strengthen relationships, foster trust, and encourage personal accountability.

LEADING THROUGH CONFLICT RESOLUTION

Conflict is natural in any workplace, especially in diverse teams with varied perspectives. Effective leaders don't avoid conflict; instead, they address it constructively, using it as an opportunity to strengthen team dynamics and foster collaboration.

1. **Conflict Resolution Techniques**:
   - **Identify the Root Cause**: Conflicts often have underlying causes that go beyond the surface issue. Asking questions and actively listening can help uncover these.
   - **Facilitate Open Dialogue**: Encourage all parties to express their views respectfully without interrupting or judging.
   - **Focus on Common Goals**: Highlight shared objectives that everyone can agree on to redirect focus from personal differences to team goals.
   - **Seek Win-Win Solutions**: Aim for resolutions where all parties feel they've gained something, fostering mutual respect and cooperation.

2. **Example**: Suppose two team members are in conflict over how to approach a project. The leader brings both

individuals together and allows each to explain their perspective. After identifying that both team members are concerned about the project's success, the leader suggests a compromise that incorporates ideas from both. By focusing on the shared goal of a successful project, the leader guides them toward a resolution that benefits the entire team.

Leaders who actively resolve conflicts help create a positive work environment, improve team cohesion, and encourage open communication.

BUILDING OPEN COMMUNICATION CHANNELS

Open communication channels encourage transparency, increase trust, and ensure that information flows freely within the organization. Leaders who foster open communication help their teams feel more comfortable sharing ideas, asking questions, and raising concerns.

1. **Ways to Build Open Communication Channels**:
   - **Regular Check-Ins**: Schedule regular one-on-one meetings or team updates to discuss progress, challenges, and feedback.
   - **Use Multiple Communication Methods**: Some team members may prefer face-to-face meetings, while others might be more comfortable communicating via email or chat platforms.
   - **Encourage Feedback**: Create a culture where feedback is welcomed and valued, whether it's positive or constructive.
   - **Lead by Example**: Be transparent with your own communications, sharing both successes and challenges, so the team knows it's safe to do the same.

2. **Example**: A leader in a growing company notices that some employees feel out of the loop about changes in

the organization. To address this, the leader introduces a monthly "town hall" meeting where company updates are shared, and employees can ask questions. Additionally, they create a dedicated Slack channel for team members to share updates and feedback. This creates multiple communication pathways, ensuring that everyone has access to the information they need.

Open communication channels lead to greater transparency, empower team members to voice their ideas, and promote a sense of belonging and engagement.

Summary

In this chapter, we've examined key communication skills that leaders must develop to be effective. From actively listening and crafting clear messages to handling difficult conversations and resolving conflicts, each skill is essential for fostering a positive and productive team environment. Leaders who communicate openly and effectively create a foundation of trust, encourage collaboration, and inspire their teams to perform at their best. Effective communication is not just a tool but a cornerstone of leadership, impacting every aspect of team dynamics and organizational success.

CHAPTER 4: DECISION-MAKING AND PROBLEM SOLVING

Effective leadership hinges on a leader's ability to make sound decisions and solve problems efficiently. Leaders are often faced with complex challenges and high-stakes decisions that can significantly impact their teams and organizations. In this chapter, we delve into frameworks for effective decision-making, explore how to balance logic and intuition, examine ways to manage risks, and highlight the importance of learning from failures. Additionally, we discuss how to foster a collaborative environment that encourages team members to participate in problem-solving.

FRAMEWORKS FOR EFFECTIVE DECISION-MAKING

Using structured frameworks for decision-making can help leaders make well-considered choices and remain consistent, even under pressure. A decision-making framework guides leaders through each step of the process, ensuring all aspects are considered and potential outcomes are weighed.

1. **The Rational Decision-Making Model**:
   - **Define the Problem**: Clearly identify the issue at hand. For example, a production delay might require analyzing why it occurred in the first place.
   - **Identify Alternatives**: List all possible solutions. This could include outsourcing work temporarily, reallocating resources, or adjusting deadlines.
   - **Evaluate the Options**: Weigh the pros and cons of each alternative, considering factors like cost, feasibility, and impact on the team.
   - **Choose and Implement the Best Option**: Select the solution that best aligns with organizational goals and execute it.
   - **Evaluate the Outcome**: After implementation, review the results to see if the solution effectively addressed the

problem. This step allows for adjustments and future improvements.

2. **Example**: Suppose a retail manager needs to decide whether to keep certain items in inventory during the off-season. By using the Rational Decision-Making Model, the manager can evaluate options, such as offering discounts to clear out stock or storing it until demand rises. The decision becomes clearer after weighing costs, potential revenue, and customer demand, ultimately leading to an informed choice that benefits the store's profitability.

Frameworks ensure a structured approach, which reduces impulsiveness and increases the likelihood of making well-rounded decisions that take multiple factors into account.

BALANCING LOGIC AND INTUITION

Effective leaders blend logical analysis with intuitive insight to make informed yet adaptable decisions. While logic provides structure and reliability, intuition—rooted in experience and instinct—allows leaders to make quick, flexible choices when time or information is limited.

1. **Logic-Based Decision-Making**:
   - Logical thinking involves using data, evidence, and critical reasoning. For example, a leader deciding on a budget allocation may analyze past performance metrics and forecasts to determine where funds would be most effective.
   - Logical decision-making is particularly useful in situations where clear data exists and time allows for thorough analysis.

2. **Intuitive Decision-Making**:
   - Intuition involves drawing from past experiences, instincts, and gut feelings. A leader might sense that a particular team member would be a great fit for a new project, even if they lack formal qualifications.
   - Intuition is essential in fast-paced or ambiguous situations where data might be incomplete, and immediate action is necessary.

3. **Example**: Consider a marketing director deciding between two advertising strategies. While the logical option, backed by analytics, may suggest a particular campaign, the director's intuition—based on years of experience—might suggest a different approach. By balancing logic with intuition, the director may choose to test both options in a small campaign before fully committing, thus harnessing both approaches to make an optimized decision.

Balancing logic and intuition helps leaders make thoughtful decisions that are both grounded in facts and adaptable to unforeseen changes or opportunities.

ANALYZING AND MANAGING RISKS

Risk is inherent in every decision. Leaders who analyze and manage risks can prepare for potential setbacks, allocate resources wisely, and protect their teams and organizations. Effective risk management involves assessing the probability and impact of various risks and creating contingency plans.

1. **Steps in Risk Analysis**:

   - **Identify Potential Risks**: Determine what could go wrong in a given situation. For example, launching a new product could carry risks related to market reception or production costs.

   - **Assess the Likelihood and Impact**: Estimate the probability of each risk occurring and the potential consequences if it does.

   - **Develop Mitigation Strategies**: Plan ways to reduce or manage the risks. For instance, if there's a high likelihood of a supplier delay, a leader might establish a backup supplier to minimize disruption.

   - **Implement and Monitor**: Put risk management strategies in place and monitor their effectiveness over time.

2. **Example**: A construction project manager anticipates potential delays due to weather. By identifying this risk, assessing its probability, and setting up an

alternative work schedule, the manager can mitigate the impact, ensuring the project remains close to schedule even in adverse conditions.

By analyzing risks, leaders can make proactive decisions that protect the organization from unforeseen setbacks, thereby fostering resilience and confidence among team members.

LEARNING FROM FAILURES AND SETBACKS

Mistakes and failures are inevitable in any leadership journey. Leaders who embrace setbacks as learning opportunities build resilience and set a powerful example for their teams. By analyzing what went wrong and identifying lessons learned, leaders can avoid repeating mistakes and continuously improve.

1. **Steps to Learning from Failures**:

     ◦ **Acknowledge the Failure**: Recognize when things have not gone as planned and take responsibility where appropriate.

     ◦ **Analyze the Root Causes**: Identify why the failure occurred. Did it stem from a lack of planning, miscommunication, or insufficient resources?

     ◦ **Identify Takeaways**: Consider what lessons can be derived from the experience. For example, if a product launch fails, lessons may involve better market research or customer feedback collection.

     ◦ **Implement Changes**: Apply what has been learned to future decisions and strategies.

2. **Example**: A tech startup releases a product with high expectations, but it underperforms in the market. The CEO analyzes customer feedback and realizes

the product lacks certain features users expect. By acknowledging this failure, studying customer needs, and incorporating this feedback into a future update, the CEO demonstrates resilience and a commitment to continuous improvement.

Embracing failures as learning opportunities enhances adaptability, innovation, and resilience, all of which are essential qualities in effective leadership.

ENCOURAGING COLLABORATIVE PROBLEM SOLVING

Effective leaders understand that complex problems are often best solved with collective input. Encouraging collaborative problem-solving fosters creativity, leverages diverse perspectives, and builds a strong sense of team ownership.

1. **Steps to Foster Collaboration:**
    - **Create an Inclusive Environment**: Encourage open dialogue where team members feel comfortable sharing ideas and feedback.
    - **Assign Roles and Responsibilities**: Clarify each team member's role to avoid confusion and ensure accountability.
    - **Encourage Diverse Perspectives**: Actively seek input from individuals with different backgrounds, skill sets, and viewpoints.
    - **Facilitate Open Discussion and Brainstorming**: Allow team members to discuss potential solutions freely, helping uncover unique ideas and approaches.

2. **Example**: When faced with a budget cut, a department head assembles the team to brainstorm cost-saving measures. By involving everyone, they receive suggestions that range from adjusting project scopes to renegotiating vendor contracts. This collaborative

approach results in a comprehensive plan that not only meets budgetary constraints but also maintains team morale and productivity.

Collaborative problem-solving leverages the strengths and insights of each team member, resulting in well-rounded solutions and stronger team unity.

SUMMARY

In this chapter, we explored key elements of decision-making and problem-solving that are essential for effective leadership. Using frameworks for structured decision-making, balancing logic and intuition, analyzing and managing risks, learning from failures, and encouraging collaborative problem-solving are all fundamental skills that help leaders make sound choices. When leaders approach decisions thoughtfully and engage their teams in solving complex problems, they create a resilient and adaptable organization that is better equipped to navigate challenges and seize opportunities. Effective decision-making is not about making flawless choices every time but about creating a framework that leads to continuous learning, improvement, and ultimately, success.

CHAPTER 5: BUILDING AND LEADING TEAMS

A leader's success is often reflected in the strength and cohesion of their team. Building a high-performing team requires a strategic approach to recruitment, an understanding of team dynamics, effective motivation, clear goal-setting, and consistent recognition. In this chapter, we'll explore the critical elements of team-building and leadership, offering practical guidance and examples on how to create a motivated, productive, and resilient team.

ASSEMBLING A HIGH-PERFORMING TEAM

The first step in creating a successful team is choosing the right individuals who not only possess the necessary skills but also align with the organization's mission and values. A high-performing team brings diverse perspectives, complementary strengths, and a shared commitment to success.

1. **Identify Core Competencies and Skills**:
   - Define the competencies required for each role within the team. For example, a marketing team may need creative thinkers, data analysts, and project managers.
   - Look for individuals who have both the technical skills and the interpersonal qualities that align with the team's goals.

2. **Prioritize Diversity and Inclusion**:
   - A diverse team brings various perspectives, which fosters creativity and innovation. Leaders should prioritize building a team with different backgrounds, experiences, and ideas.
   - Inclusivity ensures that all team members feel valued and have an opportunity to contribute, which builds trust and enhances collaboration.

3. **Example**: A project manager tasked with assembling a team for a product launch would look for individuals skilled in product development, marketing, and

customer research. However, by choosing team members from different age groups, ethnicities, and professional backgrounds, the manager ensures that the team will have fresh, innovative ideas to meet customer needs.

A leader's ability to assemble a balanced team of complementary talents is fundamental to achieving long-term success. By investing in diversity, a leader creates a well-rounded team that can address challenges from multiple perspectives.

UNDERSTANDING TEAM DYNAMICS

Team dynamics refer to the interactions and relationships among team members. A successful leader understands these dynamics and fosters an environment that encourages collaboration and positive interactions.

1. **Establish Clear Roles and Responsibilities:**

   - Clarity about individual roles minimizes misunderstandings and prevents duplication of effort. When team members know their responsibilities, they can focus on their strengths and contribute effectively.

2. **Encourage Open Communication:**

   - An open communication culture promotes transparency and trust, allowing team members to voice ideas and concerns without fear. Regular meetings, feedback sessions, and open-door policies can help cultivate this environment.

3. **Address Conflicts Constructively:**

   - Conflicts can arise in any team setting. Leaders should view conflicts as opportunities for growth by encouraging respectful dialogue and resolution. For example, if two team members disagree on a project approach, the leader can facilitate a discussion where each presents their perspective, leading to a collaborative solution.

4. **Example**: In a tech startup, team members from software development, design, and marketing frequently need to collaborate on product features. Conflicts may arise due to differing perspectives, but a leader who facilitates constructive discussions and encourages team members to see these conflicts as learning experiences creates a more resilient and innovative team environment.

Understanding team dynamics allows leaders to create a cohesive team where members work well together, openly communicate, and effectively manage conflict.

MOTIVATING AND EMPOWERING TEAM MEMBERS

Motivation and empowerment are key to ensuring that team members are engaged, productive, and feel valued. When leaders actively encourage growth and autonomy, team members become more invested in their work and take greater ownership of their responsibilities.

1. **Provide Autonomy and Ownership**:
   - Empower team members by giving them the freedom to make decisions within their areas of responsibility. Autonomy fosters accountability and creativity, as individuals feel trusted to manage their tasks.

2. **Invest in Professional Development**:
   - Leaders who support learning and development create a culture of growth. Providing opportunities for team members to attend training, workshops, or pursue new skills enhances engagement and helps the team stay competitive.

3. **Offer Constructive Feedback and Recognition**:
   - Regular feedback provides direction, while recognition reinforces positive behavior. Constructive feedback helps team members improve, and praise shows appreciation for

their efforts.

4. **Example**: A team leader at an NGO might empower a junior staff member to lead a small project, giving them a chance to practice leadership skills while providing mentorship. This empowerment not only motivates the individual but also builds their confidence and capability for future roles.

By motivating and empowering team members, leaders build a culture of trust and resilience where individuals feel motivated to perform at their best and contribute meaningfully.

SETTING GOALS AND EXPECTATIONS

Clear goals and expectations align a team's efforts with the organization's mission, providing direction and accountability. Effective goal-setting ensures that team members understand what is expected of them and can measure their progress.

1. **Establish SMART Goals**:
   - SMART goals—Specific, Measurable, Achievable, Relevant, and Time-bound—provide clear targets that are realistic and measurable. For example, instead of a vague goal like "increase sales," a SMART goal would be "increase quarterly sales by 10% within the next six months."

2. **Communicate Expectations Clearly**:
   - Leaders should clarify expectations for performance, deadlines, and deliverables. This clarity allows team members to prioritize tasks and take responsibility for meeting objectives.

3. **Align Goals with Team and Individual Strengths**:
   - Leaders should leverage each team member's strengths when assigning goals. For instance, a highly organized team member could be tasked with project planning, while a creative team member could handle brainstorming and idea generation.

4. **Example**: A nonprofit manager working on a community development project might set a SMART goal of "engaging 200 local residents in monthly workshops by the end of the year." By breaking this goal into smaller steps, the manager creates a clear roadmap for the team to follow, making progress easy to track and celebrate.

Setting clear goals and expectations provides a roadmap for the team, ensuring everyone works toward a common purpose and understands their role in achieving success.

RECOGNIZING AND REWARDING CONTRIBUTIONS

Recognition is a powerful motivator that reinforces positive behavior and shows appreciation for team members' hard work. By acknowledging achievements, leaders encourage continued commitment, boost morale, and create a positive work environment.

1. **Celebrate Milestones and Achievements**:
   - Recognize both individual and team accomplishments through celebrations or public acknowledgment. For example, a team lunch or a personalized thank-you note can significantly boost morale.

2. **Provide Incentives**:
   - Financial and non-financial rewards, such as bonuses, extra time off, or professional development opportunities, can serve as powerful motivators. Offering rewards tied to specific achievements can motivate team members to strive for excellence.

3. **Personalize Recognition**:
   - Leaders should understand how each team member prefers to be recognized, as not everyone enjoys public acknowledgment. Personalized appreciation, whether through

a one-on-one meeting or a group announcement, shows that the leader values each individual's contribution.

4. **Example**: A sales manager might reward a high-performing team member with a special bonus or time off. This tangible reward, combined with verbal praise, reinforces the team's goal-oriented culture and shows appreciation for hard work.

Recognition and rewards reinforce a culture of appreciation, making team members feel valued for their contributions and motivating them to continue their efforts toward shared goals.

SUMMARY

In this chapter, we explored the essential components of building and leading a successful team. From selecting the right team members to setting clear goals and recognizing achievements, each aspect plays a critical role in fostering a cohesive, high-performing group. Leaders who understand team dynamics, motivate and empower their members, set clear expectations, and celebrate contributions create a positive environment that drives collective success. By focusing on these foundational practices, leaders can build teams that not only meet but exceed organizational goals, creating a resilient and innovative workforce that thrives on collaboration and mutual respect.

CHAPTER 6: LEADING THROUGH CHANGE

Change is an inevitable part of any organization's journey, whether driven by market dynamics, technological advancements, or shifts in societal expectations. Leaders play a critical role in guiding their teams and organizations through change, ensuring a smooth transition while fostering adaptability and resilience. This chapter explores the nature of change within organizations, the strategies for preparing and managing it, approaches to overcoming resistance, cultivating adaptability, and leading with resilience during uncertain times.

THE NATURE OF CHANGE IN ORGANIZATIONS

Organizational change can take many forms, from minor adjustments in procedures to significant transformations in structure, strategy, or culture. Leaders must recognize the diverse types of change and understand the unique challenges that each brings to effectively guide their teams.

1. **Types of Change:**
   - **Incremental Change:** These are small, continuous improvements that organizations make to enhance processes, such as optimizing a workflow or updating software systems.
   - **Transformational Change:** This is a more radical shift, often altering the very nature of the organization, such as a merger, rebranding, or a complete overhaul of business operations.
   - **Reactive vs. Proactive Change:** Reactive change happens in response to external pressures (like competition or regulation), while proactive change is driven by innovation or future-oriented thinking.

2. **The Importance of Change:**
   - Change enables organizations to stay relevant

and competitive in rapidly evolving markets. For example, a company that continually innovates and adapts its products is more likely to thrive compared to one that resists change.

◦ Embracing change also fosters growth by helping organizations improve processes, expand capabilities, and respond effectively to market shifts.

3. **Example**: When a traditional retail company pivots to e-commerce, it must embrace both structural and cultural changes. Leaders in this scenario need to re-educate employees on digital tools, introduce new marketing strategies, and adapt customer service approaches for online platforms.

Understanding the nature of change prepares leaders to anticipate challenges, communicate effectively, and set a positive tone that helps teams embrace new directions.

PREPARING FOR AND MANAGING CHANGE

Preparation is critical to managing change effectively. Leaders must develop strategies, communicate clearly, and create support systems to ensure that changes are understood, accepted, and implemented smoothly.

1. **Developing a Clear Vision and Strategy**:
   - Define the purpose and benefits of the change clearly. This clarity ensures that all stakeholders understand the direction and importance of the shift. Leaders should develop a roadmap with specific milestones to track progress and maintain momentum.

2. **Effective Communication**:
   - Communication is key to reducing uncertainty and building trust. Leaders should keep lines of communication open, offering clear, consistent updates on progress and addressing concerns as they arise.

3. **Engaging Stakeholders**:
   - Engage everyone impacted by the change, from team members to clients. When people feel involved, they are more likely to buy into the process. Leaders can organize workshops, meetings, and forums where stakeholders can share feedback and express concerns.

4. **Building a Support Structure**:

○ Support structures, such as change management teams or mentorship programs, can help employees adapt. Leaders should identify team members who are champions of change to serve as role models and provide guidance.

5. **Example**: A tech firm transitioning to a hybrid work model might hold regular meetings to gather feedback, share updates, and address concerns. By fostering transparency and support, leaders can guide employees through the logistical and cultural changes required for the new model.

Preparation and management strategies empower leaders to guide teams through changes with confidence, clarity, and support, making transitions smoother and less disruptive.

OVERCOMING RESISTANCE TO CHANGE

Resistance is a natural reaction to change, as people often feel uncomfortable with uncertainty and the potential loss of control. Leaders must understand the roots of resistance and address it constructively to ensure a successful transformation.

1. **Understanding Sources of Resistance**:
   - **Fear of the Unknown**: Employees may fear losing their jobs, status, or control. Leaders need to address these fears by providing as much information as possible.
   - **Loss of Familiarity**: Change can disrupt routines, which can be unsettling. Leaders should acknowledge the discomfort and help team members navigate the transition.

2. **Communicating the Benefits of Change**:
   - Show how the change aligns with both organizational goals and individual aspirations. Leaders can highlight positive outcomes, like new career opportunities or skill development, to demonstrate personal and professional benefits.

3. **Encouraging Feedback and Dialogue**:
   - By providing avenues for employees to

express their concerns, leaders can identify specific issues and address them directly. This open dialogue can alleviate anxieties and build trust.

4. **Providing Training and Resources**:

    ◦ Resistance can stem from a lack of confidence in performing new tasks. Leaders can offer training sessions, resources, and ongoing support to help employees feel equipped to manage their new roles.

5. **Example**: When a company introduces a new technology system, employees might resist due to a lack of familiarity. A proactive leader could organize training sessions, demonstrate the system's benefits, and offer one-on-one support for those struggling to adapt.

Overcoming resistance to change requires empathy, communication, and practical support, all of which enable leaders to foster a more adaptable and cooperative team.

CREATING A CULTURE OF ADAPTABILITY

Adaptability is essential in today's fast-paced, ever-evolving world. Leaders who cultivate a culture of adaptability empower their teams to respond to change positively and confidently.

1. **Fostering Continuous Learning**:
   - Encourage team members to embrace a growth mindset by promoting professional development and learning opportunities. Leaders can introduce learning as a core value and incentivize skill-building efforts.

2. **Encouraging Flexibility and Innovation**:
   - By promoting open-mindedness, leaders can help their teams feel comfortable with experimentation. Leaders can organize brainstorming sessions, recognize creative solutions, and celebrate small wins to reinforce this mindset.

3. **Empowering Teams to Make Decisions**:
   - When teams have the authority to make decisions, they feel more ownership over their work and are more likely to adapt to changes quickly. Leaders should delegate responsibilities, allowing teams to adapt processes as needed.

4. **Example**: A company that regularly conducts cross-functional workshops encourages employees to

collaborate and learn from each other, fostering an adaptable culture. By promoting innovation and reducing silos, the organization can respond to changes more rapidly.

Creating a culture of adaptability prepares organizations to navigate change with agility, resilience, and confidence.

LEADING WITH RESILIENCE IN UNCERTAIN TIMES

Resilience is the capacity to recover and adapt in the face of setbacks, challenges, or crises. Leaders who demonstrate resilience serve as anchors for their teams, offering stability and assurance when circumstances are uncertain.

1. **Modeling Resilience**:
   - Resilient leaders demonstrate confidence, positivity, and persistence, even in difficult times. By setting an example, they inspire their teams to adopt a similar approach.

2. **Prioritizing Self-Care and Well-Being**:
   - Leaders who prioritize their own well-being and encourage their teams to do the same foster a supportive environment. Strategies like encouraging breaks, promoting work-life balance, and recognizing mental health challenges build a resilient workforce.

3. **Focusing on Long-Term Vision**:
   - Resilient leaders remind their teams of the bigger picture, helping them to see beyond temporary challenges. This perspective motivates teams to stay focused, even when short-term outcomes are uncertain.

4. **Encouraging a Problem-Solving Mindset**:

    ◦ Resilient leaders view challenges as opportunities for growth. By encouraging team members to see setbacks as learning experiences, they help build a more optimistic and proactive team culture.

5. **Example**: During the COVID-19 pandemic, resilient leaders who maintained regular communication, provided resources for remote work, and acknowledged team members' struggles demonstrated a strong commitment to their employees. This approach kept teams engaged, motivated, and adaptable despite unprecedented challenges.

Leading with resilience ensures that teams feel supported, empowered, and capable of facing future changes with strength and adaptability.

SUMMARY

In this chapter, we examined the essential skills and strategies for leading through change, from understanding the nature of change and preparing for transitions to overcoming resistance, creating a culture of adaptability, and leading with resilience. By embracing these principles, leaders can transform challenges into opportunities, guiding their teams with confidence and fostering an environment where change is not just managed but welcomed. In a world where change is constant, leaders who champion adaptability and resilience are well-equipped to navigate uncertainties and lead their organizations toward sustainable success.

CHAPTER 7:
DEVELOPING
FUTURE LEADERS

The foundation of any successful organization lies not only in its current leaders but also in its ability to cultivate the next generation of leaders. Developing future leaders involves identifying potential, providing guidance through mentorship, fostering a culture of continuous learning, planning for succession, and ultimately building a legacy. This chapter delves into these critical aspects, providing actionable insights and examples to equip current leaders with the tools to nurture future talent effectively.

IDENTIFYING AND NURTURING LEADERSHIP POTENTIAL

Identifying leadership potential is the first step toward cultivating future leaders. It requires a keen eye for specific traits, behaviors, and experiences that indicate a person's ability to lead effectively.

1. **Recognizing Key Traits**:
   - **Initiative**: Look for individuals who take the lead on projects or seek out opportunities to improve processes without being asked. These individuals show a proactive attitude that is essential for effective leadership.
   - **Emotional Intelligence**: Individuals who demonstrate empathy, self-awareness, and social skills are often well-suited for leadership roles. They can build strong relationships and foster a positive work environment.
   - **Resilience**: Potential leaders who can navigate setbacks and remain focused on their goals display resilience, a vital trait for any leader.

2. **Providing Opportunities for Growth**:

- Once potential leaders are identified, organizations should provide them with challenging assignments that stretch their capabilities. This could include leading a project team, managing a cross-functional initiative, or spearheading a community engagement effort.

- **Example**: A company may identify an employee in a junior role who consistently exceeds expectations. The organization can offer this individual a chance to lead a small team on a critical project, allowing them to develop their leadership skills while contributing to the organization's goals.

3. **Regular Feedback and Evaluation**:

- Implementing regular feedback mechanisms helps to assess the development of potential leaders. This can be done through performance reviews, one-on-one check-ins, and peer evaluations to provide a well-rounded perspective on their growth.

Identifying and nurturing leadership potential requires organizations to look beyond traditional markers of success, creating a pipeline of talent that aligns with their values and mission.

MENTORSHIP AND COACHING TECHNIQUES

Mentorship and coaching are vital components of leadership development, providing future leaders with the guidance and support they need to thrive.

1. **Establishing Mentorship Programs**:

   - Organizations should create structured mentorship programs that pair emerging leaders with experienced mentors. These relationships offer opportunities for learning, networking, and skill development.

   - **Example**: A large corporation may initiate a formal mentorship program where junior employees are paired with senior leaders. Regular meetings can be scheduled to discuss career goals, challenges, and strategies for growth.

2. **Coaching Techniques**:

   - Effective coaching involves setting specific goals, providing constructive feedback, and encouraging self-reflection. Leaders should ask open-ended questions that prompt future leaders to think critically about their actions and decisions.

   - **Example**: A manager could coach an aspiring

leader by asking, "What challenges did you face during this project, and how did you overcome them?" This encourages the individual to reflect on their problem-solving skills and apply those lessons to future situations.

3. **Creating a Safe Space for Growth**:
   - A supportive environment where individuals feel safe to express their thoughts and concerns is crucial for effective mentorship and coaching. Leaders should foster a culture that encourages open dialogue and acceptance of failure as part of the learning process.

4. **Diverse Mentorship**:
   - Pairing future leaders with mentors from diverse backgrounds and experiences can provide them with broader perspectives and insights, enriching their leadership journey.

By leveraging mentorship and coaching techniques, organizations can foster the personal and professional growth of future leaders, equipping them with the skills and confidence needed to succeed.

FOSTERING A LEARNING CULTURE

A culture of continuous learning is essential for developing future leaders. This culture encourages individuals to seek knowledge, share insights, and embrace challenges as opportunities for growth.

1. **Encouraging Lifelong Learning**:
    - Organizations should promote ongoing education through workshops, seminars, online courses, and certifications. Encouraging employees to pursue learning opportunities helps them stay current in their fields and develop new skills.
    - **Example**: A tech company might provide access to online courses for employees to learn new programming languages or management techniques, demonstrating a commitment to their growth.

2. **Knowledge Sharing**:
    - Create platforms for employees to share knowledge and best practices, such as lunch-and-learn sessions, internal webinars, or team discussions. This collaborative approach fosters a sense of community and encourages continuous improvement.
    - **Example**: A manufacturing firm may hold monthly meetings where employees present

lessons learned from recent projects, fostering an environment of shared learning and collective problem-solving.

3. **Encouraging Experimentation**:
   - Allowing employees to take risks and experiment without fear of failure is crucial. A culture that encourages innovation and creative problem-solving prepares future leaders to think critically and adapt to changing circumstances.
   - **Example:** A retail company might implement a pilot program where employees can propose and test new sales strategies, providing a platform for innovation and leadership development.

4. **Recognizing Learning Achievements**:
   - Celebrate learning milestones and accomplishments, whether it's completing a course or implementing a successful initiative. Recognition reinforces the value of learning and motivates others to pursue growth.

Fostering a learning culture empowers future leaders to continuously develop their skills and knowledge, positioning them for success in an ever-changing landscape.

SUCCESSION PLANNING FOR SUSTAINED LEADERSHIP

Succession planning is the process of identifying and developing potential leaders to ensure a seamless transition of leadership roles when needed. This proactive approach safeguards the organization's future and enhances its stability.

1. **Identifying Critical Roles**:
   - Organizations must identify key leadership roles and assess the skills and competencies required for each. This evaluation should consider both current needs and future strategic objectives.
   - **Example**: A healthcare organization might identify the role of Chief Medical Officer as critical and assess the skills required, such as clinical expertise and strategic thinking.

2. **Creating a Talent Pool**:
   - Develop a pool of candidates who exhibit leadership potential and align with the organization's values and goals. This pool should consist of individuals from diverse backgrounds and experiences.

- **Example**: A nonprofit organization may conduct talent assessments and identify staff members who have demonstrated leadership qualities in their current roles, adding them to the talent pool for future leadership positions.

3. **Providing Development Opportunities**:
   - Offer targeted development opportunities for individuals in the talent pool. This may include leadership training, cross-functional projects, and mentorship programs to equip them with the necessary skills.
   - **Example**: A financial institution might rotate promising employees through different departments, allowing them to gain a comprehensive understanding of the organization and develop diverse leadership skills.

4. **Regular Assessment and Feedback**:
   - Continuously assess the talent pool and provide regular feedback on development progress. This ensures that individuals remain engaged and on track for future leadership opportunities.

5. **Example**: A global corporation may have a formal succession plan that identifies key positions and outlines potential successors for each role. This approach ensures that the organization is prepared for transitions and can maintain leadership continuity.

Succession planning strengthens organizational resilience by ensuring that capable leaders are ready to step into key roles when the need arises, thus promoting sustained leadership.

BUILDING A LEGACY

Leaders who focus on developing future talent contribute to creating a lasting legacy that transcends their tenure. This legacy encompasses the values, culture, and impact they leave behind for future generations.

1. **Instilling Core Values**:
    - Leaders should articulate and exemplify the organization's core values, ensuring that future leaders understand and embody these principles. This foundational understanding shapes the culture and direction of the organization.

2. **Creating Mentorship Networks**:
    - Building mentorship networks that extend beyond formal programs creates a community of support for emerging leaders. These networks can facilitate knowledge exchange, guidance, and collaboration across the organization.

3. **Documenting Best Practices**:
    - Encourage leaders to document their experiences, insights, and lessons learned, creating a repository of knowledge that future leaders can reference. This practice ensures that valuable insights are preserved and passed on.

4. **Promoting Community Engagement**:
    - Encourage future leaders to engage

with the community and demonstrate the organization's commitment to social responsibility. This engagement fosters a sense of purpose and builds a positive reputation for the organization.

5. **Example**: A leader who champions corporate social responsibility initiatives leaves a legacy that emphasizes community engagement, inspiring future leaders to continue this commitment and fostering a culture of giving back.

By focusing on building a legacy, leaders ensure that their impact extends beyond their immediate influence, shaping the organization's culture, values, and approach for years to come.

SUMMARY

In this chapter, we explored the essential components of developing future leaders, from identifying potential and providing mentorship to fostering a learning culture, succession planning, and building a lasting legacy. By investing in the next generation of leaders, organizations can create a sustainable leadership pipeline that drives innovation, adaptability, and long-term success. Effective leadership development not only benefits individuals but also enriches the entire organization, ensuring that it remains resilient and forward-thinking in an ever-changing landscape.

By investing in the next generation of leaders, organizations not only ensure their own sustainability but also contribute positively to the broader community and industry. The commitment to developing future leaders reflects a forward-thinking mindset that prioritizes growth, adaptability, and responsibility.

DEVELOPING
FUTURE LEADERS

As we conclude this chapter, it is essential to reiterate that the art of leadership is not solely about individual success but also about fostering a community of capable, confident, and empowered leaders. By implementing strategies for identifying potential, providing effective mentorship, nurturing a culture of learning, ensuring succession planning, and building a meaningful legacy, current leaders can create an environment that champions growth and excellence.

The future of any organization rests in the hands of its leaders, and the responsibility to nurture that future is one that must be embraced by today's leaders. In doing so, they pave the way for a legacy of leadership that not only uplifts individuals but also strengthens the entire organization, ensuring it remains robust and ready to tackle the challenges of tomorrow.

REFLECTIVE QUESTIONS FOR READERS

1. **What initiatives are currently in place within your organization to identify and nurture leadership potential?**

   - Reflect on existing programs and consider how they align with best practices outlined in this chapter.

2. **How can you personally contribute to the development of future leaders within your team or organization?**

   - Identify actionable steps you can take, whether through mentorship, coaching, or creating learning opportunities.

3. **What legacy do you wish to leave as a leader?**

   - Consider how your actions today will influence future generations and the organizational culture long after you've moved on.

4. **In what ways can your organization foster a more robust learning culture?**

   - Think about specific practices or changes that could be implemented to encourage continuous learning and knowledge sharing.

5. **How does your organization approach succession planning? Are there areas for improvement?**

    ◦ Assess the effectiveness of current succession planning efforts and identify gaps that need to be addressed.

ACTION STEPS

- **Create a Development Plan**: Design a personalized development plan for yourself or for potential leaders in your organization, outlining specific goals, mentorship opportunities, and timelines.
- **Establish a Mentorship Program**: If one doesn't already exist, advocate for or initiate a mentorship program within your organization to facilitate knowledge transfer and support emerging leaders.
- **Promote Learning Opportunities**: Encourage your organization to invest in training and development resources, ensuring access to ongoing education for all employees.
- **Engage in Open Dialogues**: Foster open discussions about leadership and growth within your teams, inviting diverse perspectives and experiences that can enrich the conversation.
- **Document Success Stories**: Share and document examples of successful leadership development within your organization to inspire others and reinforce the importance of cultivating future leaders.

In closing, the journey of leadership development is continuous and multifaceted. As we embrace the responsibility of nurturing future leaders, we enrich not only our organizations but also the communities in which we operate. By championing the principles discussed in this chapter, we can ensure a robust pipeline of leaders ready to navigate the complexities of the future with confidence, vision, and integrity.

The impact of today's leadership decisions will resonate far into the future, and each of us has a role to play in shaping that legacy. Through dedicated effort and strategic planning, we can unlock the full potential of our teams, ensuring a vibrant, dynamic, and resilient organizational culture for generations to come.

CHAPTER 8: ETHICS AND INTEGRITY IN LEADERSHIP

In an era marked by rapid change and complexity, ethical leadership stands as a cornerstone of effective leadership practice. Leaders not only drive organizational performance but also shape the ethical climate of their organizations. This chapter delves into the importance of ethical leadership, the processes involved in making ethical decisions, the significance of fostering an ethical culture, the roles of accountability and transparency, and strategies for handling ethical dilemmas.

THE IMPORTANCE OF ETHICAL LEADERSHIP

Ethical leadership is the practice of being honest and virtuous in a role as a leader. It encompasses making decisions that align with the core values of the organization while also considering the broader impact on stakeholders, including employees, customers, and the community. The importance of ethical leadership cannot be overstated for several reasons:

1. **Trust Building**: Ethical leaders foster trust among employees and stakeholders. When leaders demonstrate integrity and uphold ethical standards, they inspire confidence in their teams, enhancing collaboration and morale. Trust is fundamental for a positive organizational culture, enabling open communication and innovation.

   - **Example**: A CEO who openly addresses challenges within the organization and is transparent about decision-making processes fosters a culture of trust, encouraging employees to voice their opinions without fear of retaliation.

2. **Reputation Management**: Organizations led by ethical leaders are better positioned to maintain a positive reputation. In the age of social media, public scrutiny is intense; unethical behavior can quickly lead to public relations crises that can damage an organization's brand and customer loyalty.

- ◦ **Example**: Companies like Patagonia, which prioritize environmental responsibility and ethical sourcing, have built strong reputations that resonate with consumers, leading to sustained success.

3. **Long-Term Success**: Ethical leadership contributes to long-term organizational success. While unethical decisions might yield short-term gains, they often lead to long-term repercussions, including legal challenges, employee turnover, and loss of customer trust.

- ◦ **Example**: Volkswagen's emissions scandal demonstrated how unethical leadership decisions can result in billions in fines, loss of market share, and irreversible damage to brand reputation.

4. **Compliance and Risk Mitigation**: Ethical leaders are vigilant about compliance with laws and regulations, reducing the risk of legal issues and financial penalties. They ensure that ethical standards are integrated into business practices and that employees are trained to recognize and adhere to these standards.

- ◦ **Example**: An organization that implements regular ethics training and compliance audits can proactively prevent violations and create an ethical framework for operations.

MAKING ETHICAL DECISIONS

Making ethical decisions involves a thoughtful process that weighs the potential impacts on stakeholders and aligns actions with organizational values. Here are the key components of ethical decision-making:

1. **Identify the Ethical Issues**: The first step in ethical decision-making is to recognize the ethical dimensions of a situation. Leaders must be aware of how their choices affect others and what principles are at stake.

   ○ **Example**: A manager may face an ethical dilemma when deciding whether to report a colleague's unethical behavior. Recognizing the implications of both reporting and not reporting is crucial.

2. **Gather Relevant Information**: Leaders should collect all pertinent facts and consider the context of the decision. This includes understanding the perspectives of different stakeholders and the potential outcomes of various actions.

   ○ **Example**: Before implementing a cost-cutting measure, a leader should gather data on how it will affect employee morale and customer satisfaction.

3. **Evaluate Options**: Leaders must consider the possible alternatives and evaluate them against ethical principles such as fairness, respect, and justice. This

process often involves asking critical questions:

- Who will be affected by this decision?
- Are there conflicting values at play?
- What would I want to happen if I were on the receiving end of this decision?
- **Example**: When faced with layoffs, a leader should weigh the financial benefits against the emotional and social impacts on employees and their families.

4. **Make the Decision**: After evaluating options, leaders should choose the course of action that aligns best with ethical principles and organizational values. It is essential to communicate the rationale behind the decision transparently.

   - **Example**: A leader deciding to implement a diversity hiring initiative should articulate the reasons behind this choice, emphasizing the value of inclusion and representation in the workplace.

5. **Reflect on the Outcome**: After the decision has been made and implemented, leaders should reflect on the results. Did the decision uphold ethical standards? What lessons were learned that can inform future decisions?

   - **Example**: Following a significant organizational change, leaders should assess employee feedback and performance metrics to evaluate the ethical implications of their choices.

BUILDING AN ETHICAL CULTURE

Creating an ethical culture within an organization is crucial for ensuring that ethical behavior is not only encouraged but also expected. An ethical culture serves as a guiding framework for decision-making and behavior at all levels of the organization.

1. **Establishing Core Values**: Organizations should define their core values and ensure they are clearly communicated throughout the organization. These values should guide behavior and decision-making, setting the tone for an ethical culture.

    ◦ **Example**: A financial institution may adopt values such as integrity, accountability, and customer focus, integrating them into every aspect of its operations.

2. **Leadership Commitment**: Leaders play a pivotal role in establishing and maintaining an ethical culture. Their commitment to ethical practices must be evident in their actions and decisions. Leaders should model ethical behavior and encourage employees to do the same.

    ◦ **Example**: A company's leadership team could participate in community service projects, demonstrating a commitment to social responsibility and encouraging employees to engage in similar initiatives.

3. **Training and Education**: Organizations should

provide training on ethical behavior, decision-making processes, and compliance with regulations. Regular workshops and discussions can help reinforce ethical principles and equip employees with the tools to navigate ethical dilemmas.

- ◦ **Example**: A tech company might offer annual ethics training sessions that cover topics such as data privacy, conflict of interest, and responsible AI use.

4. **Open Communication**: Fostering an environment where employees feel safe discussing ethical concerns is vital. Organizations should implement mechanisms for reporting unethical behavior, such as anonymous hotlines or open-door policies.

- ◦ **Example**: A healthcare organization may establish a confidential reporting system that allows employees to report unethical behavior without fear of retaliation.

5. **Rewarding Ethical Behavior**: Recognizing and rewarding ethical behavior reinforces the importance of ethics within the organization. Leaders should celebrate employees who demonstrate integrity and uphold the organization's values.

- ◦ **Example**: A company might introduce an "Ethics Champion" award to acknowledge employees who exemplify ethical conduct and contribute to the organization's ethical culture.

By actively building and nurturing an ethical culture, organizations empower their employees to make ethical decisions and prioritize integrity in their daily actions.

ACCOUNTABILITY AND TRANSPARENCY

Accountability and transparency are crucial elements of ethical leadership. Leaders must hold themselves and others accountable for their actions while fostering an environment of openness.

1. **Setting Clear Expectations**: Leaders should establish clear standards of behavior and communicate these expectations to employees. This clarity helps individuals understand what is required of them and the consequences of unethical behavior.

    ○ **Example**: A manufacturing company might publish a code of conduct that outlines expected behaviors and procedures for reporting violations.

2. **Encouraging Ownership**: Leaders should empower employees to take ownership of their actions and decisions. This involves creating a culture where individuals feel responsible for their contributions and are encouraged to learn from mistakes.

    ○ **Example**: A project manager might encourage team members to openly discuss failures during project reviews, fostering a culture of accountability and continuous improvement.

3. **Transparent Decision-Making**: Leaders should strive for transparency in their decision-making processes. When employees understand the reasoning behind

decisions, they are more likely to trust and support those choices.

- Example: A nonprofit organization may publicly share its decision-making process for allocating resources, helping stakeholders understand how funds are used.

4. **Feedback Mechanisms**: Organizations should implement feedback mechanisms that allow employees to express concerns and provide input on ethical practices. Regular surveys, focus groups, and open forums can facilitate this process.

- Example: A retail company could conduct annual employee surveys to gauge perceptions of ethical practices and identify areas for improvement.

5. **Addressing Violations**: When ethical violations occur, leaders must address them promptly and transparently. This may involve disciplinary action, public acknowledgment of the issue, and steps taken to prevent recurrence.

- Example: If a company discovers misconduct, its leadership should publicly communicate the findings and outline the measures taken to rectify the situation, reinforcing the commitment to ethical standards.

By prioritizing accountability and transparency, leaders can build trust within their organizations and create an environment where ethical behavior is not only expected but celebrated.

HANDLING ETHICAL DILEMMAS

Despite best efforts, leaders will inevitably face ethical dilemmas. Handling these challenges effectively requires a structured approach to decision-making and a commitment to ethical principles.

1. **Recognizing Ethical Dilemmas**: The first step in addressing an ethical dilemma is recognizing it as such. Leaders should be aware of situations where competing values or interests may create conflicts.

   ◦ **Example**: A manager may face a dilemma when asked to cut costs by reducing employee benefits, conflicting with the value of employee welfare.

2. **Gathering Perspectives**: In ethical dilemmas, it's important to consider the perspectives of all stakeholders involved. Engaging in discussions with team members can provide valuable insights and help identify potential solutions.

   ◦ **Example**: Before making a decision regarding layoffs, a leader might hold discussions with affected employees to understand their concerns and perspectives.

3. **Weighing Alternatives**: Leaders should evaluate the potential outcomes of various options while considering ethical principles. This involves weighing the pros and cons of each choice against the

organization's core values.

- ◦ **Example**: A marketing team may need to decide whether to exaggerate product benefits in advertising. Leaders should consider the ethical implications of misleading customers versus the potential financial gains from such advertising.

4. **Consulting Ethical Frameworks**: Utilizing established ethical frameworks can guide leaders through dilemmas. Frameworks such as utilitarianism (maximizing overall happiness), deontological ethics (focusing on duties and rights), and virtue ethics (considering moral character) can provide clarity.

- ◦ **Example**: A leader facing a dilemma about whether to disclose a data breach may analyze the situation through a utilitarian lens, assessing the greater good for customers and the organization versus the short-term impacts of transparency.

5. **Making a Decision and Taking Action**: After thoroughly evaluating the situation, leaders must make a decision. It's important to take responsibility for that decision and act upon it swiftly to mitigate any negative consequences.

- ◦ **Example**: If a leader decides to address an ethical breach by implementing corrective actions, they should communicate the decision to all stakeholders, clarifying the rationale and expected outcomes.

6. **Learning from the Experience**: After resolving an ethical dilemma, leaders should reflect on the process and outcomes to extract lessons that can inform future decision-making. This reflection helps to improve the organization's approach to ethical issues.

- **Example**: A company might conduct a post-mortem analysis of an ethical dilemma to understand what went wrong and how similar situations can be better handled in the future.

7. **Creating a Support System**: Establishing a network of trusted advisors or an ethics committee can provide leaders with support when faced with tough decisions. This system can offer diverse perspectives and help in navigating complex ethical challenges.

- **Example**: A healthcare organization may form an ethics committee to consult on sensitive issues such as patient privacy and resource allocation, ensuring that multiple viewpoints are considered before making decisions.

By equipping themselves with strategies for handling ethical dilemmas, leaders can navigate complex situations with confidence and integrity, reinforcing their commitment to ethical principles and strengthening the organization's ethical culture.

ETHICS AND INTEGRITY IN LEADERSHIP

Ethics and integrity are indispensable components of effective leadership. Leaders set the tone for their organizations by exemplifying ethical behavior and fostering a culture that prioritizes integrity, accountability, and transparency. The impact of ethical leadership extends beyond individual organizations, influencing broader societal values and expectations.

As leaders navigate the complexities of decision-making and organizational dynamics, they must remain steadfast in their commitment to ethical principles. By recognizing the importance of ethical leadership, making informed ethical decisions, building a culture of integrity, and effectively addressing ethical dilemmas, leaders can create organizations that thrive on trust, respect, and responsibility.

The commitment to ethics is not merely an obligation but an opportunity for leaders to make a profound impact on their organizations and society as a whole. As this chapter concludes, let it serve as a reminder that ethical leadership is not a destination but a continuous journey, one that requires vigilance, reflection, and dedication to fostering a positive legacy for future generations.

ACTION STEPS

- **Assess and Align Values**: Take time to review your personal and organizational values. Ensure that they align, and consider how you can better integrate them into your leadership style.

- **Implement Ethical Training**: Advocate for or initiate ethics training programs within your organization, focusing on real-world scenarios that employees may encounter.

- **Create Open Channels for Discussion**: Establish regular forums or meetings where employees can discuss ethical concerns openly without fear of repercussions.

- **Develop a Personal Ethics Policy**: Create a personal ethics policy outlining your principles and how you intend to uphold them as a leader. Share this with your team to promote transparency.

- **Engage in Continuous Learning**: Stay informed about ethical practices in your industry and participate in workshops or seminars that enhance your understanding of ethics in leadership.

FINAL THOUGHTS

Ethical leadership is a commitment to integrity, transparency, and accountability. In an ever-evolving landscape of challenges and opportunities, the principles outlined in this chapter provide a foundation for leaders to navigate ethical complexities with confidence. By fostering an ethical culture, making principled decisions, and addressing dilemmas with care, leaders can not only achieve organizational goals but also leave a lasting legacy of ethical excellence for future generations to emulate.

CHAPTER 9:
LEVERAGING TECHNOLOGY AND INNOVATION

In the rapidly evolving landscape of modern leadership, technology and innovation play pivotal roles. Leaders who effectively harness these elements not only enhance their organizational capabilities but also position themselves as forward-thinking influencers in their fields. This chapter explores the multifaceted relationship between leadership, technology, and innovation, examining the essential skills and strategies leaders must cultivate to thrive in an increasingly digital world.

THE ROLE OF TECHNOLOGY IN MODERN LEADERSHIP

Technology has transformed the way leaders operate, communicate, and make decisions. In today's interconnected environment, effective leaders leverage technology to enhance collaboration, streamline processes, and improve decision-making. The following points illustrate the key roles of technology in leadership:

1. **Enhancing Communication**: Advanced communication tools, such as video conferencing, instant messaging, and collaborative platforms, enable leaders to maintain clear and consistent communication with their teams, regardless of geographical barriers.

    ○ **Example**: A remote team spread across different countries can hold daily stand-up meetings using video conferencing tools like Zoom, fostering a sense of connection and alignment.

2. **Facilitating Collaboration**: Technology allows teams to collaborate in real-time, share information seamlessly, and work together on projects. This fosters innovation and enhances productivity.

    ○ **Example**: Tools like Slack or Microsoft Teams enable team members to collaborate on projects through shared channels, file sharing, and real-time discussions.

3. **Data-Driven Decision-Making**: Technology provides leaders with access to vast amounts of data, allowing them to make informed decisions based on insights rather than intuition alone.

   ◦ **Example**: A retail manager can analyze customer purchasing patterns through data analytics software to optimize inventory and improve sales strategies.

4. **Improving Efficiency**: Automation and other technological innovations can streamline repetitive tasks, allowing leaders to focus on strategic initiatives that drive growth.

   ◦ **Example**: Utilizing customer relationship management (CRM) systems can automate follow-up emails, enabling sales teams to prioritize more complex client interactions.

5. **Enhancing Customer Engagement**: Digital technologies enable leaders to engage with customers more effectively, providing personalized experiences that foster loyalty and satisfaction.

   ◦ **Example**: Companies like Amazon use advanced algorithms to recommend products based on previous customer behavior, enhancing the shopping experience.

EMBRACING DIGITAL TRANSFORMATION

Digital transformation is not just about adopting new technologies; it involves a fundamental shift in how organizations operate and deliver value. Leaders must be champions of this transformation, guiding their teams through the changes that accompany digital innovation. The following strategies can aid leaders in embracing digital transformation:

1. **Cultivating a Digital Mindset**: Leaders should foster a culture that encourages experimentation, adaptability, and learning. This mindset helps teams embrace digital tools and approaches.

    ○ **Example**: A leader might promote hackathons or innovation days, where team members can explore new technologies and propose digital solutions to existing challenges.

2. **Investing in Technology**: Leaders need to assess their current technology stack and invest in tools that align with their strategic goals. This may involve upgrading existing systems or adopting entirely new platforms.

    ○ **Example**: A manufacturing firm might invest in IoT (Internet of Things) devices to improve supply chain efficiency and reduce downtime through predictive maintenance.

3. **Aligning Technology with Strategy**: Leaders should ensure that their technology investments align with their organizational strategy. Technology should

enable and enhance business objectives, not hinder them.

- ◦ **Example**: A nonprofit organization aiming to expand its outreach may implement digital marketing tools to increase its visibility and engagement with potential donors.

4. **Empowering Teams**: Leaders should empower their teams to leverage digital tools and technologies effectively. Providing training and resources enables employees to utilize technology to its full potential.

- ◦ **Example**: A company might offer workshops on data analytics tools, equipping team members with the skills to analyze and interpret data for better decision-making.

5. **Measuring Impact**: Tracking the impact of digital transformation initiatives is crucial. Leaders should establish metrics to assess how technology adoption contributes to organizational goals.

- ◦ **Example**: A company may track key performance indicators (KPIs) such as customer satisfaction scores and operational efficiency metrics to gauge the success of its digital initiatives.

ENCOURAGING INNOVATIVE THINKING

Innovation is the lifeblood of successful organizations. Leaders must create an environment that nurtures creativity and encourages innovative thinking among team members. Here are strategies to foster innovation:

1. **Creating a Safe Space for Ideas**: Leaders should cultivate an environment where employees feel comfortable sharing their ideas without fear of criticism. This encourages open dialogue and creativity.

   - **Example**: Implementing regular brainstorming sessions where all team members can contribute ideas can lead to fresh perspectives and innovative solutions.

2. **Promoting Diversity of Thought**: Diverse teams bring different experiences and perspectives, fostering creativity. Leaders should actively seek to build diverse teams and leverage their collective strengths.

   - **Example**: A tech startup might prioritize hiring individuals from various backgrounds, ensuring a broad range of ideas and solutions to problems.

3. **Providing Resources for Experimentation**: Leaders should allocate resources, such as time and funding,

for teams to experiment with new ideas and concepts. This encourages a culture of innovation.

> ○ **Example**: A company may allocate a portion of its budget for research and development, allowing teams to prototype new products or services.

4. **Recognizing and Rewarding Innovation**: Acknowledging and rewarding innovative contributions can motivate employees to continue thinking creatively. Leaders should celebrate successes and learn from failures.

> ○ **Example**: Implementing an innovation award or recognition program can encourage team members to share and pursue their innovative ideas.

5. **Encouraging Cross-Functional Collaboration**: Bringing together individuals from different departments can spark innovative thinking. Leaders should promote cross-functional teams to tackle specific challenges.

> ○ **Example**: A healthcare organization may create cross-functional teams to design new patient care processes, combining expertise from clinical, administrative, and IT departments.

USING DATA FOR INFORMED LEADERSHIP

Data-driven decision-making is critical in modern leadership. Leaders must be adept at utilizing data to inform their strategies and initiatives. Here are ways leaders can harness data effectively:

1. **Establishing Data Literacy**: Leaders should ensure that their teams possess the necessary skills to analyze and interpret data. This may involve providing training and resources.

   - **Example**: A financial services firm may conduct workshops on data analytics tools, enabling employees to make data-informed decisions in their roles.

2. **Investing in Analytics Tools**: Leaders should invest in analytics tools that provide insights into customer behavior, market trends, and operational efficiency.

   - **Example**: A retail company might implement advanced analytics platforms to analyze customer purchasing patterns and optimize inventory management.

3. **Integrating Data Across Departments**: Data silos can hinder decision-making. Leaders should encourage cross-departmental collaboration to ensure data is shared and integrated effectively.

- ◦ **Example**: A marketing team might collaborate with sales to analyze customer feedback data, enabling them to refine marketing strategies.

4. **Utilizing Predictive Analytics**: Leaders should leverage predictive analytics to anticipate future trends and make proactive decisions.

- ◦ **Example**: A manufacturing company may use predictive analytics to forecast equipment failures, allowing them to schedule maintenance proactively and reduce downtime.

5. **Fostering a Culture of Continuous Improvement**: Leaders should promote a culture that values data-driven insights and encourages continuous improvement based on data analysis.

- ◦ **Example**: An organization may establish regular review sessions to analyze performance data and identify areas for improvement.

STAYING AGILE IN A TECHNOLOGICAL WORLD

In a rapidly changing technological landscape, agility is essential for effective leadership. Leaders must adapt quickly to new challenges and opportunities. The following strategies can help leaders stay agile:

1. **Adopting Agile Methodologies**: Implementing agile methodologies enables leaders to respond to change quickly and efficiently. Agile frameworks encourage iterative processes and continuous feedback.

   - **Example**: A software development team using Agile methodologies can adapt to changing client requirements by regularly revisiting and adjusting project plans.

2. **Encouraging Flexibility and Adaptability**: Leaders should promote a culture of flexibility, encouraging teams to pivot quickly in response to changes in the market or customer needs.

   - **Example**: A consumer goods company may rapidly shift its product line to meet changing consumer preferences during economic downturns.

3. **Investing in Continuous Learning**: Staying updated on technological trends and developments is crucial. Leaders should foster a culture of continuous learning

within their organizations.

- ○ **Example**: A leader might encourage team members to take online courses related to emerging technologies, ensuring the organization remains competitive.

4. **Monitoring Industry Trends**: Keeping an eye on industry trends and technological advancements allows leaders to anticipate changes and capitalize on new opportunities.

- ○ **Example**: A healthcare organization may track advancements in telemedicine to enhance patient care and accessibility.

5. **Building Resilience**: Leaders should cultivate resilience within their teams, encouraging them to embrace challenges and learn from setbacks.

- ○ **Example**: During a crisis, a leader can facilitate debriefing sessions to reflect on lessons learned and strategize for future challenges.

In conclusion, the integration of technology and innovation into leadership practices is not just beneficial; it is essential for success in today's fast-paced environment. Effective leaders leverage technology to enhance communication, facilitate collaboration, and make informed decisions. By embracing digital transformation, encouraging innovative thinking, utilizing data, and remaining agile, leaders can navigate the complexities of the modern world and drive their organizations toward sustainable growth.

As technology continues to advance, leaders must adapt and evolve their leadership styles to incorporate these changes. The key to successful leadership lies in a proactive approach to technology and innovation, fostering a culture of continuous improvement, and remaining committed to ethical principles in all endeavors.

By taking these steps, leaders will not only empower their teams but also position themselves and their organizations as pioneers in their respective fields. In the ever-changing landscape of technology and innovation, the ability to lead effectively becomes synonymous with the ability to embrace change. This chapter underscores that successful leadership today is not merely about maintaining the status quo but about anticipating the future and preparing teams to meet it head-on.

INTEGRATING THE LESSONS

To effectively leverage technology and innovation, leaders must integrate these lessons into their daily practices. Here's how they can apply the principles discussed in this chapter:

1. **Fostering a Culture of Innovation**: Leaders should actively promote an organizational culture that encourages innovation at every level. This involves recognizing and rewarding creative efforts and ensuring that all team members feel empowered to share their ideas.

2. **Investing in Training and Development**: Continuous learning is crucial in a rapidly changing technological landscape. Leaders can facilitate training programs that focus on emerging technologies and innovative practices, helping their teams stay ahead of the curve.

3. **Encouraging Feedback and Open Communication**: Creating channels for open feedback allows teams to voice concerns and share insights about technology and innovation. Leaders should regularly solicit input on how technology is impacting their work and encourage discussions about improvements.

4. **Balancing Technology with Human Touch**: While technology can streamline processes and enhance efficiency, effective leadership also requires a human touch. Leaders should ensure that technology serves to enhance interpersonal relationships and not replace

them, fostering a collaborative environment that values human connections.

5. **Monitoring Trends and Being Proactive**: Staying informed about industry trends and technological advancements is critical. Leaders should allocate time for research and networking to understand emerging technologies that could impact their organizations.

REAL-WORLD EXAMPLES OF EFFECTIVE TECHNOLOGICAL LEADERSHIP

To further illustrate the concepts in this chapter, here are a few real-world examples of organizations and leaders who have successfully leveraged technology and innovation:

- **Microsoft**: Under the leadership of Satya Nadella, Microsoft underwent a significant cultural transformation. Nadella emphasized the importance of a growth mindset and encouraged employees to embrace technology through initiatives that promoted continuous learning and collaboration. Microsoft's transition to cloud computing exemplified how effective leadership can pivot an organization toward innovation.

- **Tesla**: Elon Musk's leadership at Tesla showcases the power of innovation in a highly competitive industry. By prioritizing research and development, Tesla has consistently pushed the boundaries of electric vehicle technology, inspiring a movement toward sustainable energy solutions. Musk's approach encourages teams to take risks and embrace failure as part of the innovation process.

- **Airbnb**: In response to the COVID-19 pandemic, Airbnb's leadership rapidly adapted its business model, focusing on local experiences and long-term stays. This agility in response to changing market demands highlights how leaders can leverage technology to pivot and innovate, ensuring the organization remains relevant.

Final Thought

As we move further into an era defined by rapid technological advancement, the need for leaders who can effectively harness the power of technology and innovation will only grow. Effective leadership in this context requires not only technical acumen but also the ability to inspire and engage teams in embracing these changes.

By leveraging technology to enhance communication, collaboration, and decision-making, leaders can create organizations that are not only resilient but also capable of thriving in the face of uncertainty. As this chapter concludes, it serves as a reminder that the future of leadership is inherently tied to our ability to innovate, adapt, and lead with integrity in an ever-evolving landscape.

In the following chapters, we will continue to explore essential elements of effective leadership, building on the foundation established in this chapter to delve deeper into the art and science of leadership. As leaders, it is crucial to remain open-minded and ready to embrace new ideas, ensuring that we continue to grow alongside the technology and innovations shaping our world.

THE ROLE OF TECHNOLOGY IN MODERN LEADERSHIP

Technology is no longer just an operational tool; it has become a strategic asset that shapes how organizations function and compete. Leaders must understand the various technological tools available and how they can be utilized to enhance productivity, improve decision-making, and foster innovation.

- **Reflection Question**: What technologies are currently impacting your organization, and how are they influencing your leadership approach?

EMBRACING DIGITAL TRANSFORMATION

Digital transformation is about rethinking business processes, enhancing customer experiences, and creating value through technology. Leaders play a pivotal role in guiding their organizations through this transformation by setting clear goals and communicating the vision effectively.

- **Reflection Question**: How are you preparing your team for digital transformation, and what steps are you taking to ensure they are equipped to adapt?

ENCOURAGING INNOVATIVE THINKING

Innovation is not solely the responsibility of a dedicated team; it should be embedded in the organization's culture. Leaders must create an environment where employees feel safe to experiment, fail, and learn from their mistakes. Encouraging innovative thinking involves recognizing and rewarding creativity while also providing the necessary resources for exploration.

- **Reflection Question**: In what ways are you currently fostering a culture of innovation within your team? What barriers to creativity might exist, and how can you address them?

USING DATA FOR INFORMED LEADERSHIP

Data-driven decision-making is critical for effective leadership. Leaders should leverage data analytics to gain insights into performance metrics, customer preferences, and market trends. This approach enables more informed decisions that can drive strategic initiatives and improve organizational performance.

- **Reflection Question**: How are you currently utilizing data in your decision-making process, and what tools or techniques can you implement to enhance this practice?

STAYING AGILE IN A TECHNOLOGICAL WORLD

The rapid pace of technological change demands agility from leaders. Staying ahead of trends and being willing to pivot when necessary is essential. Agile leadership involves adapting strategies quickly in response to new information or changing circumstances.

- **Reflection Question**: How do you respond to unexpected challenges or changes in your industry? Are there specific strategies you can adopt to increase your agility as a leader?

INTEGRATING THE LESSONS

To effectively leverage technology and innovation, leaders must integrate these lessons into their daily practices. Here's how they can apply the principles discussed in this chapter:

1. **Fostering a Culture of Innovation**: Leaders should actively promote an organizational culture that encourages innovation at every level. This involves recognizing and rewarding creative efforts and ensuring that all team members feel empowered to share their ideas.

    ◦ **Reflection Question**: How can you recognize and reward innovative ideas within your organization to encourage more creativity?

2. **Investing in Training and Development**: Continuous learning is crucial in a rapidly changing technological landscape. Leaders can facilitate training programs that focus on emerging technologies and innovative practices, helping their teams stay ahead of the curve.

    ◦ **Reflection Question**: What training programs or learning opportunities can you implement to enhance your team's skills in technology and innovation?

3. **Encouraging Feedback and Open Communication**: Creating channels for open feedback allows teams to voice concerns and share insights about technology and innovation. Leaders should regularly solicit input

on how technology is impacting their work and encourage discussions about improvements.

- ◦ **Reflection Question**: What mechanisms do you currently have in place to encourage open communication and feedback within your team?

4. **Balancing Technology with Human Touch**: While technology can streamline processes and enhance efficiency, effective leadership also requires a human touch. Leaders should ensure that technology serves to enhance interpersonal relationships and not replace them, fostering a collaborative environment that values human connections.

- ◦ **Reflection Question**: How can you ensure that technology enhances rather than diminishes personal connections within your team?

5. **Monitoring Trends and Being Proactive**: Staying informed about industry trends and technological advancements is critical. Leaders should allocate time for research and networking to understand emerging technologies that could impact their organizations.

- ◦ **Reflection Question**: What steps can you take to stay informed about the latest trends and technologies in your industry?

REAL-WORLD EXAMPLES OF EFFECTIVE TECHNOLOGICAL LEADERSHIP

To further illustrate the concepts in this chapter, here are a few real-world examples of organizations and leaders who have successfully leveraged technology and innovation:

- **Microsoft**: Under the leadership of Satya Nadella, Microsoft underwent a significant cultural transformation. Nadella emphasized the importance of a growth mindset and encouraged employees to embrace technology through initiatives that promoted continuous learning and collaboration. Microsoft's transition to cloud computing exemplified how effective leadership can pivot an organization toward innovation.

- **Reflection Question**: What lessons can you draw from Microsoft's transformation under Satya Nadella, and how might they apply to your leadership style?

- **Tesla**: Elon Musk's leadership at Tesla showcases the power of innovation in a highly competitive industry. By prioritizing research and development, Tesla has consistently pushed the boundaries of electric vehicle technology, inspiring a movement toward sustainable energy solutions. Musk's approach encourages teams to take risks and embrace failure as part of the innovation process.

- **Reflection Question**: How does Tesla's focus on innovation and risk-taking influence your understanding of leadership in a competitive environment?

- **Airbnb**: In response to the COVID-19 pandemic, Airbnb's leadership rapidly adapted its business model, focusing on local experiences and long-term stays. This agility in response to changing market demands highlights how leaders can leverage technology to pivot and innovate, ensuring the organization remains relevant.

- **Reflection Question**: In what ways can you cultivate adaptability within your team to respond to unexpected changes in your industry?

FINAL THOUGHTS

As we move further into an era defined by rapid technological advancement, the need for leaders who can effectively harness the power of technology and innovation will only grow. Effective leadership in this context requires not only technical acumen but also the ability to inspire and engage teams in embracing these changes.

By leveraging technology to enhance communication, collaboration, and decision-making, leaders can create organizations that are not only resilient but also capable of thriving in the face of uncertainty. As this chapter concludes, it serves as a reminder that the future of leadership is inherently tied to our ability to innovate, adapt, and lead with integrity in an ever-evolving landscape.

In the following chapters, we will continue to explore essential elements of effective leadership, building on the foundation established in this chapter to delve deeper into the art and science of leadership. As leaders, it is crucial to remain open-minded and ready to embrace new ideas, ensuring that we continue to grow alongside the technology and innovations shaping our world.

CHAPTER 10: PERSONAL GROWTH AND SELF-CARE FOR LEADERS

Leadership is a demanding role that requires not only the ability to guide and inspire others but also the capability to reflect on one's own strengths, weaknesses, and well-being. As leaders navigate challenges and responsibilities, prioritizing personal growth and self-care becomes essential. This chapter explores the significance of self-awareness, strategies for personal development, the balance between work and life, and the importance of mindfulness and continual learning.

THE IMPORTANCE OF SELF-AWARENESS

Self-awareness is the foundation of effective leadership. It involves understanding one's emotions, strengths, weaknesses, values, and the impact of one's behavior on others. Leaders who possess high self-awareness are better equipped to make informed decisions, communicate effectively, and build strong relationships with their teams.

1. **Understanding Emotions**: Leaders must recognize their emotions and how these emotions influence their reactions and decision-making. For instance, a leader who understands their stress triggers can manage their responses during high-pressure situations.

   - **Reflection Question**: What emotions do you find most challenging to manage in your leadership role, and how do these emotions affect your interactions with your team?

2. **Receiving Feedback**: Seeking feedback from peers, mentors, and team members is crucial for developing self-awareness. Constructive criticism can illuminate blind spots and provide insights into areas for improvement.

   - **Reflection Question**: How often do you seek feedback from others about your leadership style, and what steps do you take to incorporate that feedback into your growth?

3. **Identifying Core Values**: Leaders who understand their core values can lead with authenticity and integrity. Aligning decisions and actions with these values fosters trust and respect from team members.

   ◦ **Reflection Question**: What are your core values as a leader, and how do they guide your decision-making process?

STRATEGIES FOR PERSONAL GROWTH

Leaders must actively engage in personal growth to remain effective and resilient. Here are several strategies that can facilitate this process:

1. **Setting Personal Goals**: Like organizational objectives, personal goals provide direction and motivation. Leaders should identify specific areas for growth, such as improving communication skills, enhancing emotional intelligence, or developing strategic thinking.

   ◦ **Reflection Question**: What specific personal goals have you set for your leadership development, and how do you plan to achieve them?

2. **Seeking Mentorship**: Engaging with mentors or coaches can accelerate personal growth. These relationships offer guidance, support, and new perspectives that challenge leaders to expand their thinking and skills.

   ◦ **Reflection Question**: Who are the mentors in your life, and how have they contributed to your development as a leader?

3. **Participating in Workshops and Training**: Continuous education through workshops, seminars, and training sessions exposes leaders to new ideas and best practices, fostering skill development and

innovation.

- **Reflection Question**: What recent training or workshop have you attended, and how has it influenced your approach to leadership?

WORK-LIFE BALANCE AND AVOIDING BURNOUT

Maintaining a healthy work-life balance is critical for leaders to avoid burnout and sustain their effectiveness. Leaders must prioritize their well-being to be able to lead others effectively.

1. **Setting Boundaries**: Establishing clear boundaries between work and personal life is vital. Leaders should communicate their availability to team members and stick to those boundaries to ensure time for rest and personal pursuits.

   ○ **Reflection Question**: How do you currently set boundaries between your work and personal life, and what changes could you make to improve that balance?

2. **Delegating Responsibilities**: Effective leaders understand that they cannot do everything themselves. Delegating tasks not only empowers team members but also allows leaders to focus on strategic priorities.

   ○ **Reflection Question**: Are there tasks you can delegate to others on your team to free up time for your priorities and self-care?

3. **Taking Breaks**: Regular breaks throughout the day can boost productivity and mental well-being. Leaders should incorporate short breaks to recharge and

prevent fatigue.

- **Reflection Question**: How often do you take breaks during your workday, and how do these breaks impact your overall productivity and mindset?

MINDFULNESS AND STRESS MANAGEMENT

In today's fast-paced work environment, leaders must cultivate mindfulness and stress management techniques to remain grounded and focused.

1. **Practicing Mindfulness**: Mindfulness involves being present and fully engaged in the moment. Leaders can practice mindfulness through techniques such as meditation, deep breathing, or simply taking a moment to pause and reflect during the day.

    - **Reflection Question**: How do you incorporate mindfulness practices into your daily routine, and how do they affect your leadership effectiveness?

2. **Identifying Stressors**: Leaders should identify their primary stressors and develop strategies to mitigate them. This could involve time management techniques, seeking support from colleagues, or engaging in hobbies outside of work.

    - **Reflection Question**: What are your top stressors as a leader, and what proactive measures can you take to address them?

3. **Promoting Well-Being in the Workplace**: Leaders can foster a culture of well-being within their organizations by encouraging team members to

practice self-care, offering resources for mental health support, and promoting a healthy work-life balance.

- **Reflection Question**: How can you promote well-being among your team members, and what resources or initiatives could you implement to support their mental health?

CONTINUAL LEARNING AND DEVELOPMENT

In a rapidly changing world, continual learning is essential for leaders to stay relevant and effective.

1. **Embracing Lifelong Learning**: Leaders should adopt a mindset of lifelong learning, actively seeking opportunities to acquire new skills and knowledge. This can include reading books, taking online courses, or attending industry conferences.

   ○ **Reflection Question**: What steps are you taking to engage in lifelong learning, and how has it impacted your leadership capabilities?

2. **Encouraging Team Development**: Leaders should also invest in their team's development by providing access to training, mentorship, and professional growth opportunities. This not only enhances the team's skills but also boosts morale and retention.

   ○ **Reflection Question**: How do you support your team's professional development, and what additional resources could you provide to enhance their growth?

3. **Reflecting on Experiences**: Regular reflection on experiences allows leaders to extract valuable lessons and insights. Leaders should take time to evaluate their decisions, successes, and failures, using these

reflections to inform future actions.

- **Reflection Question**: How often do you take time to reflect on your leadership experiences, and what insights have you gained from this practice.

In conclusion, personal growth and self-care are integral to effective leadership. By cultivating self-awareness, setting goals, managing work-life balance, practicing mindfulness, and embracing continual learning, leaders can enhance their effectiveness while maintaining their well-being. This chapter serves as a reminder that leadership is not solely about guiding others but also about nurturing oneself. As leaders prioritize their personal development and well-being, they position themselves to lead with authenticity, resilience, and effectiveness in a complex and ever-changing world.

CONCLUSION

Leadership is a multifaceted journey that encompasses various skills, experiences, and lessons learned over time. As we reach the end of this guide, it is crucial to reflect on the key leadership lessons, the ongoing journey of development, the importance of inspiring others, and the overarching theme of embracing the art of leadership.

Summing Up Key Leadership Lessons

Throughout this guide, we have explored essential principles and practices that contribute to effective leadership. Here are some of the key lessons:

1. **The Power of Self-Awareness**: Understanding oneself is the cornerstone of effective leadership. Self-aware leaders can manage their emotions, recognize their strengths and weaknesses, and engage with their teams authentically.

2. **The Importance of Adaptability**: The landscape of leadership is ever-changing. Successful leaders are those who can adapt their styles and approaches to meet the needs of their teams and the demands of their environment.

3. **Communication is Key**: Effective communication fosters trust, collaboration, and clarity. Leaders must master the art of active listening and articulate their messages clearly to ensure that everyone is on the same page.

4. **Decision-Making is a Skill**: Leaders are constantly faced with decisions that impact their teams and

organizations. Utilizing a structured decision-making framework while balancing logic and intuition is vital for making sound choices.

5. **Empowering Others**: Leadership is not just about directing; it's about empowering team members. By motivating and recognizing the contributions of others, leaders can create a high-performing culture that drives success.

6. **Ethics and Integrity Matter**: Ethical leadership fosters a culture of accountability and transparency. Leaders must prioritize ethical decision-making and create an environment where integrity is valued.

7. **The Role of Technology**: Embracing technology and innovation is essential in today's fast-paced world. Leaders must leverage technological advancements to enhance efficiency, communication, and collaboration.

8. **Self-Care is Essential**: Leaders who prioritize their well-being can perform more effectively and sustainably. Practicing self-care, mindfulness, and maintaining a work-life balance is critical to avoiding burnout.

These lessons serve as a foundation for developing effective leadership practices that can be applied in various contexts and environments.

THE JOURNEY OF LIFELONG LEADERSHIP DEVELOPMENT

Leadership is not a destination but rather a continuous journey. The commitment to lifelong learning and development is essential for every leader. As leaders progress in their careers, they must remain open to new ideas, feedback, and experiences that shape their understanding of leadership.

1. **Embrace Change**: The ability to adapt and learn from experiences, both positive and negative, is crucial. Leaders should view challenges as opportunities for growth and continually seek to enhance their skills and knowledge.

2. **Seek New Experiences**: Actively pursuing new roles, responsibilities, or projects can provide valuable learning opportunities. Leaders should not shy away from stepping out of their comfort zones to broaden their perspectives.

3. **Networking and Collaboration**: Building relationships with other leaders, mentors, and peers can provide fresh insights and diverse viewpoints. Engaging with a network of professionals can inspire new ideas and foster collaborative problem-solving.

4. **Reflection and Self-Assessment**: Regularly reflecting

on one's experiences and assessing leadership performance helps identify areas for improvement and growth. This practice encourages self-awareness and accountability.

Ultimately, the journey of leadership development is personal and unique to each individual. By embracing a mindset of growth, leaders can navigate their paths with resilience and purpose.

INSPIRING OTHERS THROUGH LEADERSHIP

Effective leadership extends beyond personal growth; it involves inspiring and motivating others to reach their full potential. Leaders who lead with passion and authenticity can create a ripple effect, positively impacting their teams and organizations.

1. **Lead by Example**: Demonstrating the values and behaviors you wish to see in your team can inspire others to follow suit. Whether it's through integrity, hard work, or collaboration, leading by example sets the standard for the entire team.

2. **Cultivate a Vision**: Articulating a compelling vision helps rally team members around a common goal. Leaders who can communicate a clear and inspiring vision motivate their teams to strive for excellence.

3. **Recognize Achievements**: Celebrating successes, both big and small, fosters a positive culture and motivates team members. Recognition encourages individuals to continue performing at their best and contributes to a sense of belonging.

4. **Empower Others**: Providing opportunities for team members to take on leadership roles, make decisions, and contribute ideas empowers them and enhances their confidence and engagement.

By inspiring others, leaders create a collaborative and innovative environment where individuals feel valued and motivated to contribute to shared goals.

FINAL THOUGHTS: EMBRACING THE ART OF LEADERSHIP

In conclusion, embracing the art of leadership involves recognizing that it is a dynamic and evolving process. Effective leadership is not solely about authority or position; it is about influencing and inspiring others while continuously striving for personal and collective growth.

1. **Cultivate Passion**: Passion for leadership is essential. Leaders who are genuinely enthusiastic about their work and the success of their teams create a positive atmosphere that fosters engagement and innovation.

2. **Be Open to Change**: The willingness to adapt and embrace change is a hallmark of effective leadership. As the world evolves, so too must leaders' approaches, strategies, and mindsets.

3. **Nurture Relationships**: Building strong relationships with team members and stakeholders is crucial. Trust and collaboration are essential components of effective leadership that lead to enhanced performance and success.

4. **Never Stop Learning**: The journey of leadership is ongoing. Leaders must remain committed to learning and self-improvement, actively seeking opportunities for growth and development.

By embodying these principles and lessons, leaders can navigate the complexities of their roles while creating meaningful impact in their organizations and communities. Leadership is indeed an art—one that requires practice, reflection, and a genuine desire to inspire and uplift others. Embrace this art, and you will unlock the potential not only within yourself but also within those you lead.

EFFECTIVE LEADERSHIP: A GUIDE FOR UNLOCKING THE ART OF LEADERSHIP, REFLEXIVE QUESTIONS WORKSHEET

Chapter	Reflective Questions	Your Responses
Chapter 1: The Foundation of Leadership	1. What does leadership mean to you personally, and how does your definition align with the core principles discussed in this chapter?	

	2. Reflect on a leader you admire. What vision, mission, and values did they embody, and how did these contribute to their effectiveness?	
	3. How do you currently assess your emotional intelligence, and in what ways can you enhance it to improve your leadership capabilities?	
	4. Describe a situation where trust and credibility were crucial. How did you establish or rebuild trust in that scenario?	
Chapter 2: Leadership Styles and When to Use Them	1. Which leadership style do you naturally gravitate toward, and how does it impact your effectiveness as a leader?	
	2. Think of a time when you had to adapt your	

	leadership style to fit a specific situation. What was the outcome, and what did you learn?	
	3. How do you incorporate elements of servant leadership into your current role, and how does it affect your team's performance?	
	4. Can you identify a context in which you could have applied a different leadership style? What changes would you implement in future situations?	
Chapter 3: Communic ation Skills for Leaders	1. How would you rate your active listening skills, and what specific actions can you take to improve them?	
	2. Reflect on a challenging conversation you've had. How did you handle it, and what could you have done	

	differently?	
	3. In what ways do you ensure that your messages are clear and effective? What barriers do you face in communication?	
	4. Think of a time when conflict arose within your team. How did you approach resolving it, and what were the results?	
Chapter 4: Decision-Making and Problem Solving	1. Describe a decision you made recently. What frameworks or criteria did you use to guide your decision-making process?	
	2. How do you balance logic and intuition in your decision-making? Can you recall a situation where this balance was critical?	
	3. Reflect on a risk you took that didn't go as planned. What did you learn from that experience, and	

	how can you apply those lessons in the future?	
	4. How do you foster collaboration when solving problems with your team? What practices have been most effective?	
Chapter 5: Building and Leading Teams	1. What do you consider the key qualities of a high-performing team, and how do you cultivate those qualities within your team?	
	2. Reflect on a time when understanding team dynamics led to a successful outcome. What insights did you gain?	
	3. How do you motivate and empower your team members? Can you identify areas for improvement in your approach?	
	4. In what ways do you recognize and reward	

	contributions from your team? How do these actions impact team morale and performance?	
Chapter 6: Leading Through Change	1. How do you personally respond to change, and how does that affect your leadership during transitional periods?	
	2. What strategies do you employ to prepare your team for change, and how effective have they been?	
	3. Reflect on a situation where you encountered resistance to change. How did you address it, and what was the outcome?	
	4. In what ways do you encourage a culture of adaptability in your organization? What challenges do you face in fostering this culture?	

Chapter 7: Developing Future Leaders	1. How do you identify leadership potential in others? Can you share a specific example from your experience?	
	2. What mentorship or coaching techniques have you found to be most effective in developing future leaders?	
	3. How do you create a learning culture within your organization, and what benefits have you observed from it?	
	4. Reflect on your own legacy as a leader. What do you want to be remembered for, and how are you actively building that legacy?	
Chapter 8: Ethics and Integrity in Leadership	1. Why do you believe ethical leadership is essential? How do your values align	

	with the ethical standards you set as a leader?	
	2. Reflect on an ethical dilemma you faced. How did you navigate it, and what did you learn from the experience?	
	3. In what ways do you actively promote accountability and transparency within your team or organization?	
	4. How do you handle situations where ethical considerations may conflict with organizational goals or pressures?	
Chapter 9: Leveraging Technology and Innovation	1. How has technology influenced your leadership style and practices? Can you provide specific examples?	
	2. What challenges do you face in embracing digital	

	transformation, and how do you address them?	
	3. Reflect on a time when you encouraged innovative thinking within your team. What were the results, and how can you build on that experience?	
	4. How do you use data to inform your leadership decisions? What tools or resources do you find most valuable?	
Chapter 10: Personal Growth and Self-Care for Leaders	1. How do you cultivate self-awareness in your leadership journey? What practices or tools do you use for reflection?	
	2. What strategies do you implement for your personal growth, and how do they enhance your effectiveness as a leader?	
	3. Reflect on your	

	work-life balance. What steps can you take to improve it and avoid burnout?	
	4. How do you integrate mindfulness and stress management into your routine? What benefits have you experienced from these practices?	

APPENDICES

The appendices serve as valuable supplementary materials designed to enhance your understanding and application of the concepts covered in this guide. They provide practical resources, tools, and examples that can be utilized for further exploration of effective leadership.

Appendix A: Recommended Leadership Resources

In this section, you'll find a curated list of books, articles, podcasts, and online resources that delve deeper into various aspects of leadership. These materials are aimed at helping you expand your knowledge and gain different perspectives on leadership practices.

1. **Books:**
    - *"Leaders Eat Last" by Simon Sinek*: This book explores how leaders can create an environment of trust and cooperation in their organizations.
    - *"Dare to Lead" by Brené Brown*: Brown's work focuses on the importance of vulnerability and courage in leadership.
    - *"Good to Great" by Jim Collins*: A classic in leadership literature, it analyzes what differentiates successful companies from their mediocre counterparts.

2. **Articles:**
    - Harvard Business Review has numerous articles on leadership topics ranging from decision-making to team dynamics. Some

recommended reads include "What Makes a Leader" by Daniel Goleman and "The Authenticity Paradox" by Herminia Ibarra.

- "Leadership That Gets Results" by Daniel Goleman provides insights into different leadership styles and their impacts on organizational culture.

3. **Podcasts**:

- *"The Learning Leader Show"*: Hosted by Ryan Hawk, this podcast features interviews with top leaders and explores their experiences and insights on effective leadership.
- *"How I Built This"*: NPR's Guy Raz interviews entrepreneurs and leaders, focusing on their journeys and the leadership lessons learned along the way.

4. **Online Resources**:

- **LinkedIn Learning**: Offers various online courses on leadership skills, emotional intelligence, and team management.
- **Coursera**: Provides access to courses from universities worldwide on topics like leadership theory and organizational behavior.

Appendix B: Self-Assessment Tools for Leaders

Self-assessment tools are essential for leaders to gain insight into their strengths, weaknesses, and leadership styles. Utilizing these tools can facilitate personal growth and development. Here are a few self-assessment tools you may find useful:

1. **360-Degree Feedback**: This tool gathers feedback from peers, subordinates, and supervisors, providing a comprehensive view of one's leadership abilities. Many organizations implement this process to foster a culture of feedback and continuous improvement.

2. **Myers-Briggs Type Indicator (MBTI)**: Understanding your personality type can significantly enhance your leadership effectiveness. The MBTI helps leaders identify their communication styles, decision-making approaches, and areas for development.

3. **Emotional Intelligence (EQ) Assessments**: Tools like the EQ-i 2.0 help leaders evaluate their emotional intelligence levels, which are critical for effective leadership. High emotional intelligence contributes to better relationship management and team dynamics.

4. **StrengthsFinder**: This assessment helps individuals identify their unique strengths and talents, allowing them to leverage these qualities for greater leadership effectiveness.

5. **Leadership Practices Inventory (LPI)**: Developed by James Kouzes and Barry Posner, this tool assesses leadership practices based on their five exemplary practices of leadership.

Appendix C: Case Studies in Leadership

Case studies provide real-world examples of effective leadership practices and challenges faced by leaders across different industries. Analyzing these cases can offer valuable lessons and insights into successful leadership strategies. Below are a few notable case studies:

1. **Satya Nadella at Microsoft**: Under Nadella's leadership, Microsoft underwent a cultural transformation focused on empathy, collaboration, and innovation. This case study examines how his inclusive leadership style and emphasis on learning contributed to revitalizing the company.

2. **Howard Schultz at Starbucks**: Schultz's commitment to creating a strong corporate culture centered on employee well-being and customer experience has positioned Starbucks as a leader in the industry. This

case study explores how his values-driven approach shaped the company's success.

3. **Indra Nooyi at PepsiCo**: Nooyi's tenure as CEO was marked by a focus on sustainability and social responsibility. The case study analyzes her strategic vision and commitment to diversity, which helped reshape PepsiCo's brand and market approach.

4. **Mary Barra at General Motors**: As the first female CEO of a major global automaker, Barra navigated challenges related to safety and innovation. This case study highlights her leadership approach during crises and her vision for transforming GM into a leader in electric vehicles.

5. **Nelson Mandela's Leadership in South Africa**: This case study examines Mandela's transformative leadership during and after apartheid, focusing on his commitment to reconciliation and nation-building, emphasizing the importance of ethical leadership.

Appendix D: Leadership Development Programs and Certifications

Investing in leadership development programs and certifications can significantly enhance your skills and credentials as a leader. Here are some reputable programs and certifications that can support your growth:

1. **Center for Creative Leadership (CCL)**: Offers various leadership development programs tailored for different levels, including executive coaching and workshops focused on key leadership competencies.

2. **Kellogg School of Management**: Provides executive education programs focusing on leadership, strategy, and innovation. Their offerings include the Executive Leadership Program, which combines academic rigor with practical application.

3. **Harvard Business School Online**: Their leadership

courses, such as "Leadership Principles," combine theory and practice to equip leaders with the skills to inspire and lead teams effectively.

4. **International Coaching Federation (ICF)**: Offers certifications for coaches that can enhance your leadership skills. Becoming an ICF-certified coach enables you to lead with a coaching mindset, promoting the development of others.

5. **Project Management Institute (PMI)**: Their Project Management Professional (PMP) certification is recognized globally and enhances leadership skills, particularly in managing teams and projects effectively.

6. **American Management Association (AMA)**: Provides a variety of workshops and courses on leadership development, team management, and communication skills, catering to leaders at all levels.

The appendices of this guide aim to enrich your journey toward effective leadership. By leveraging the recommended resources, engaging with self-assessment tools, studying real-life case studies, and pursuing leadership development programs, you can enhance your understanding of leadership and apply these insights to your professional endeavors. Remember that leadership is a continual learning process, and these tools can support your growth as you unlock the art of leadership.

REFERENCES

This section includes a comprehensive list of resources that can further enhance your understanding of effective leadership. By referring to these books, articles, journals, online resources, and tools, you can expand your knowledge and apply various leadership principles in your professional journey.

Books, Articles, and Journals

Books and articles provide foundational knowledge, insights, and different perspectives on leadership. Here is a selection of key texts and articles that can serve as valuable references:

1. **Books:**
   - **"Leaders Eat Last" by Simon Sinek**: Sinek argues that true leadership is about putting others first and fostering an environment of trust and cooperation within organizations.
   - **"Dare to Lead" by Brené Brown**: This book emphasizes the significance of vulnerability, courage, and authenticity in leadership, encouraging leaders to create a culture where people feel safe to take risks.
   - **"The Five Dysfunctions of a Team" by Patrick Lencioni**: Lencioni identifies common pitfalls that teams face and offers actionable insights on building a cohesive team through trust, accountability, and commitment.

2. **Articles:**
   - **"What Makes a Leader" by Daniel Goleman**: Published in the Harvard Business Review,

this article discusses the importance of emotional intelligence in effective leadership.

- **"The Authenticity Paradox" by Herminia Ibarra**: This article explores the balance between authenticity and adaptability in leadership, highlighting the challenges leaders face in remaining genuine while navigating different situations.
- **"Leadership That Gets Results" by Daniel Goleman**: Goleman describes various leadership styles and their impact on organizational performance, emphasizing the need for emotional intelligence in adapting one's leadership approach.

3. **Journals**:

- **Leadership Quarterly**: A premier journal dedicated to publishing scholarly research on leadership theory, practice, and development. It provides empirical studies and theoretical insights into leadership behaviors and effectiveness.
- **Journal of Business Ethics**: This journal addresses ethical issues in leadership and management, offering research articles and case studies that explore ethical decision-making in organizations.
- **Harvard Business Review**: A valuable source of articles, case studies, and insights on various aspects of leadership, organizational behavior, and management strategies.

Online Resources and Tools

The digital landscape offers a wealth of resources that can aid in your leadership journey. Below are some recommended online resources and tools:

1. **Websites**:
   - **Center for Creative Leadership (CCL)**: Offers a plethora of resources, including research papers, articles, and leadership development programs designed to enhance leadership skills.
   - **Harvard Business Publishing**: Provides articles, case studies, and tools related to leadership and management, along with access to their extensive catalog of books.
   - **MindTools**: A comprehensive website that offers articles, templates, and resources on various leadership and management topics, including decision-making, team management, and personal development.

2. **Webinars and Online Courses**:
   - **Coursera**: Offers various leadership courses from renowned universities, covering topics such as emotional intelligence, strategic leadership, and organizational change.
   - **LinkedIn Learning**: Provides a wide range of video tutorials on leadership skills, team management, and personal development from industry experts.
   - **edX**: Features online courses from top institutions on leadership principles, management strategies, and related fields, allowing for flexible learning opportunities.

3. **Social Media and Networking**:
   - **LinkedIn**: A professional networking platform where leaders share insights, articles, and connect with peers. Joining leadership groups can facilitate discussions and knowledge exchange.

- **Twitter**: Follow thought leaders in the field of leadership and management to stay updated on the latest trends, articles, and discussions.

Index

The index is designed to provide a quick reference to key terms, concepts, and topics covered in this guide. It allows readers to locate specific information efficiently and enhances the usability of the book.

The references section serves as an essential resource for leaders seeking to deepen their understanding of effective leadership practices. By exploring the recommended books, articles, journals, online resources, and tools, you can gain valuable insights that will aid your journey toward becoming an effective and inspiring leader. The index further enhances the usability of this guide, allowing readers to quickly locate specific topics of interest. Remember, leadership is an ongoing learning process, and these resources will support your growth and development as you navigate the complexities of leading others.

USAGE
INSTRUCTIONS

- **Review the Questions**: Take time to read through each reflective question.
- **Respond**: Use the "Your Responses" column to jot down your thoughts, experiences, and insights related to each question.
- **Reflect**: After completing your responses, reflect on the patterns and insights you've identified about your leadership style and practices.

This worksheet format encourages active engagement with the material, promoting deeper reflection and personal growth in leadership skills.

www.ingramcontent.com/pod-product-compliance
Lightning Source LLC
Chambersburg PA
CBHW072158290526
45794CB00004B/1568